LITERARY GEOGRAPHY

Literary Geography provides an introduction to work in the field, making the interdiscipline accessible and visible to students and academics working in literary studies and human geography, as well as related fields such as the geohumanities, place writing and geopoetics.

Emphasising the long tradition of work with literary texts in human geography, this volume:

- provides an overview of literary geography as an interdiscipline, which combines aims and methods from human geography and literary studies
- explains how and why literary geography differs from spatially-oriented critical approaches in literary studies
- reviews geographical work with literary texts from the late 19th century to the present day
- includes a glossary of key terms and concepts employed in contemporary literary geography.

Accessible and clear, this comprehensive overview is an essential guide for anyone interested in learning more about the history, current activity and future of work in the interdiscipline of literary geography.

Sheila Hones is a Professor Emerita of the University of Tokyo, Japan.

THE NEW CRITICAL IDIOM
SERIES EDITOR: JOHN DRAKAKIS, UNIVERSITY OF STIRLING

The New Critical Idiom is an invaluable series of introductory guides to today's critical terminology. Each book:

- provides a handy, explanatory guide to the use (and abuse) of the term;
- offers an original and distinctive overview by a leading literary and cultural critic;
- relates the term to the larger field of cultural representation.

With a strong emphasis on clarity, lively debate and the widest possible breadth of examples, *The New Critical Idiom* is an indispensable approach to key topics in literary studies.

Race
Martin Orkin with Alexa Alice Joubin

Trauma
Stef Craps and Lucy Bond

Children's Literature
Carrie Hintz

Pastoral
Second edition
Terry Gifford

Fantasy
Lucie Armitt

Intertextuality
Third edition
Graham Allen

Literary Geography
Sheila Hones

For more information about this series, please visit: www.routledge.com/The-New-Critical-Idiom/book-series/SE0155

LITERARY GEOGRAPHY

Sheila Hones

LONDON AND NEW YORK

Cover image: 'Tube Map' by Kyle Bean

First published 2022
by Routledge
4 Park Square, Milton Park, Abingdon, Oxon OX14 4RN

and by Routledge
605 Third Avenue, New York, NY 10158

Routledge is an imprint of the Taylor & Francis Group, an informa business

© 2022 Sheila Hones

The right of Sheila Hones to be identified as author of this work has been asserted in accordance with sections 77 and 78 of the Copyright, Designs and Patents Act 1988.

All rights reserved. No part of this book may be reprinted or reproduced or utilised in any form or by any electronic, mechanical, or other means, now known or hereafter invented, including photocopying and recording, or in any information storage or retrieval system, without permission in writing from the publishers.

Trademark notice: Product or corporate names may be trademarks or registered trademarks, and are used only for identification and explanation without intent to infringe.

British Library Cataloguing in Publication Data
A catalogue record for this book is available from the British Library

Library of Congress Cataloging-in-Publication Data
Names: Hones, Sheila, author.
Title: Literary geography / Sheila Hones.
Description: New York City : Routledge, 2022. |
Series: The new critical idiom | Includes bibliographical references and index.
Identifiers: LCCN 2021053246 | ISBN 9781138013247 (hardback) |
ISBN 9781138013346 (paperback) | ISBN 9781315778273 (ebook)
Subjects: LCSH: Human geography and literature. | Space and time in literature.
Classification: LCC PN56.H764 H66 2022 | DDC 809.9335--dc23/eng/20220203
LC record available at https://lccn.loc.gov/2021053246

ISBN: 978-1-138-01324-7 (hbk)
ISBN: 978-1-138-01334-6 (pbk)
ISBN: 978-1-315-77827-3 (ebk)

DOI: 10.4324/9781315778273

Typeset in Times New Roman
by Taylor & Francis Books

Contents

Acknowledgements vi
Series Editor's Preface vii

Introduction 1

1 **Origins** 23

2 **Aims and Methods** 44

3 **Genres** 64

4 **Mappings** 86

5 **Representation** 107

6 **Futures** 126

Glossary 139

Bibliography 172
Index 188

Acknowledgements

Although I am now sometimes referred to in print as 'the geographer Sheila Hones' I am a geographer only by adoption, and so my first thanks go to all the real geographers who have helped me to read, write and think somewhat geographically. In particular, I would like to thank Lawrence Berg, Ian Cook, Mike Crang, Marcus Doel, Julian Holloway, Rob Kitchin and James Kneale. In the course of my undergraduate and postgraduate studies in American literature I benefited greatly from the guidance of William Hutchings, John Conron and William L. Vance. I would also like to express my debt of gratitude to generations of literary geographers, including (of course) Marc Brosseau, while also thanking in particular my colleagues past and present at the journal *Literary Geographies*: Juha Ridanpää, Angharad Saunders, James Kneale, Neal Alexander, David Cooper, Brigid Magner, Alexander Beaumont and David McLaughlin. In the course of the long process of writing this book I relied heavily on the support and advice of geographers Richard Carter-White and James Thurgill, while Kristen Deiter, Graham Law, Eric Magrane and Deborah Snow Molloy also read and commented on drafts. Adam Hill provided essential help in accessing materials. I am glad to have another opportunity to thank my colleagues at the University of Tokyo, especially Yujin Yaguchi. Finally, I am grateful to the series editor of the New Critical Idiom, John Drakakis, and Polly Dodson and Zoe Meyer at Taylor & Francis.

SERIES EDITOR'S PREFACE

The New Critical Idiom is a series of introductory books which seeks to extend the lexicon of literary terms, in order to address the radical changes which have taken place in the study of literature during the last decades of the 20th century. The aim is to provide clear, well-illustrated accounts of the full range of terminology currently in use, and to evolve histories of its changing usage.

The current state of the discipline of literary studies is one where there is considerable debate concerning basic questions of terminology. This involves, among other things, the boundaries which distinguish the literary from the non-literary; the position of literature within the larger sphere of culture; the relationship between literatures of different cultures; and questions concerning the relation of literary to other cultural forms within the context of interdisciplinary studies.

It is clear that the field of literary criticism and theory is a dynamic and heterogeneous one. The present need is for individual volumes on terms which combine clarity of exposition with an adventurousness of perspective and a breadth of application. Each volume will contain as part of its apparatus some indication of the direction in which the definition of particular terms is likely to move, as well as expanding the disciplinary boundaries within which some of these terms have been traditionally contained. This will involve some re-situation of terms within the larger field of cultural representation, and will introduce examples from the area of film and the modern media in addition to examples from a variety of literary texts.

INTRODUCTION

Literary geography today is an interdisciplinary practice combining and connecting work in human geography and in literary studies. Bringing together aims and methods from the humanities and the social sciences, it has its roots in two academic traditions: a long history of geographical interest in literary texts, and a more recent interest in geography and spatiality within literary studies. The complex history of the interdiscipline means that present-day literary geography embraces a wide variety of approaches, from the mapping of literary place references, to the deployment of spatial theory in close critical reading, to creative place writing. The coherence of literary geography as an interdiscipline comes from its four-way structure: the 'literary' refers to literary texts and also to literary studies, while the 'geography' includes not only geographies of the lived world and spatial concepts but also human geography as an academic discipline. While this four-way structure provides stability and purpose to the interdiscipline, variety in aims and methods means that the field as a whole can be difficult to define. It can also be difficult to appreciate how and why literary geography differs from the range of spatially-oriented critical approaches which have developed within literary studies over the past several decades. The aim of this book is to provide readers with a framework that will enable them to understand the various ways in which literary geography is being practised today. It will clarify the distinctiveness of contemporary literary geography, summarise its history and range of current practices, and highlight some of the directions in which it seems likely to develop.

LITERARY GEOGRAPHY

Before the turn of the 21st century, the question of what literary geography was and what it did was mainly a matter for geographers, who took it for granted that literary geography was a subfield of human geography. Before the mid-1970s, geographical work with literature was variously labelled ('landscape in literature', for example, or 'geography and literature'), but the field eventually became consolidated as 'literary geography' after Ramesh Dhussa established the term first in his 1976 MA thesis and then more influentially in his 'Literary geography: a bibliography' published in the *Journal of Cultural Geography* in 1981. In this era geographers were building on a long tradition of work with literary texts in human and cultural geography, while literary studies as a whole had not yet turned toward questions of space, place, landscape and geography. As late as 2009 geographer Marc Brosseau was able to define literary geography as 'the geographical analysis of fictive literature' (212), and in 2013, Juha Ridanpää summarised literary geography for *Oxford Bibliographies* as a longstanding subfield of human and cultural geography, noting that for geographers literature has been 'an object of study, a thematic context for research, a perspective through which the world is perceived [and] a methodological tool' for over a century, with work 'following the main epistemological and theoretical turns within the fields of human and cultural geographies' (2013: online). Human geography today is characterised not so much by a particular subject matter as by the way it approaches a wide range of topics and activities by reference to concepts such as space, scale, mobility, representation, process and performance. These topics include the writing and reading of literary texts.

The emphasis here on the geographical origins of literary geography is not to suggest that there was no input from literary studies in the era when it was primarily a subfield of human geography. Although it was rare in the early years for literary critics to be directly involved in collaborative work with human geographers, published work in literary criticism has routinely been consulted by literary geographers. What this means is that even when early forms of literary geography are viewed primarily as a geographical subfield, the project has always been inherently interdisciplinary, and there have always been important contributions to the field from literary studies. Today, with increased direct collaboration from scholars working in literary studies and other fields (including cartography, geopoetics, place writing and the geohumanities), literary geography is becoming a more actively collaborative interdiscipline. If, as Neal Alexander has suggested, geographers have over the past several decades become 'increasingly sophisticated readers of literary texts' (2015a: 4) then the increased collaboration now taking place in literary geography suggests that scholars coming to the field from literary studies will in turn develop an increasingly sophisticated understanding of human geography.

LITERARY GEOGRAPHIES

The plural form 'literary geographies' is used as the title for the interdisciplinary journal for work in literary geography to signal its intent to function as a broadly inclusive venue for a spectrum of work which includes but also extends beyond the interdiscipline of literary geography. Designed as a 'forum for new research and collaboration in the field of literary/geographical studies', the journal 'features work combining topics and methods from literary studies, cultural geography, cartography, and spatial theory' and recognises 'that the term "literary geography" [...] has multiple meanings and is practised in a variety of ways within different academic traditions' (*Literary Geographies* website). By using the more inclusive plural form, *Literary Geographies* indicates that it publishes work which runs from a more geographical form at one end, through a strongly interdisciplinary centre (literary geography), to a more literary form at the other. In other words, 'literary geographies' refers to a broader range of work than the singular form 'literary geography', which (at least for geographers) is generally understood to refer to an expanded form of the deep tradition in geographical work with literary texts, now benefiting from increased direct collaboration with scholars working in literary studies and other fields.

The book series *Early Modern Literary Geographies* (OUP) also uses the plural in its title, but without the centre/spectrum structure and the explicit interdisciplinarity marked by the title of the journal. The phrasing of the book series title also suggests that it is primarily interested in the historical geography of the early modern period and its literary texts. As the series overview available on the publisher's website explains, literary scholars, 'influenced by the work of cultural and human geographers', are now looking at the way people in the early modern era 'constructed their senses of the world out of interactions among places, spaces, and embodied practices' (OUP website). It further explains that the term 'literary geographies' should 'be understood capaciously' and that the editors 'invite submissions on any form of early modern writing that engages with the topics of space, place, landscape and environment'. So while the journal and the book series both use the plural term, one is more concerned with an ongoing interdisciplinary literary/geographical project and the other with a thematic approach to early modern literary studies which involves an interest in the historical geographies of the period.

OTHER DEFINITIONS OF LITERARY GEOGRAPHY

The form of literary geography at the centre of the interdisciplinary project which led to the founding of the journal *Literary Geographies* started out as a set of themes and research techniques in human geography which came together as a recognised subfield under the title 'literary geography' in the mid-1970s. After the mid-1980s, however, as this form of literary geography was expanding to include greater input from literary studies, several alternative definitions of the term 'literary geography' were proposed.

(I) LITERARY GEOGRAPHY AS A TEXTUAL FEATURE

In some cases, 'literary geography' has been defined as a textual feature rather than as an analytical approach. Leonard Kriegel, for example, in his 1994 article 'Geography lessons' for the *Sewanee Review*, emphasised the importance of an author's 'evocation of place' and the lack of critical attention that had so far been paid to that aspect of writing, pointing out that

> literary geography – by which I mean the writer's focus on place as place – has less to do with the actual shape place assumes in the mind than it does with how the idea of place feeds the imagination.
> (Kriegel, 1994: 604)

More recently, Neil Alexander has used 'literary geography' to refer both to the literary/geographical interdiscipline and to the geographical work of texts themselves, as when he notes that some of 'the most engrossing literary geographies of the past three decades are to be found in contemporary landscape writing, non-fiction prose texts that are centrally concerned with the relationships between self and place, nature and culture' (Alexander, 2015b: 1).

(II) LITERARY GEOGRAPHY AND LITERARY HISTORY

In outlining 'a conceptual literary geography of Australia' for *Australian Literary Studies* in 1991, Martin Leer defined literary geography as 'the complementary dimension to literary history, as space is the other side of time', arguing that while geographers and historians 'have long used imaginative literature as a chief source of documentation for the way human beings through the ages have perceived their natural environment', literary scholars 'have tended to be wary of geography' and have limited themselves to 'rather innocent comments on "landscape"' (Leer, 1991: 1). In a somewhat related sense, the book series *American Tropics: Towards a Literary Geography* is described on the Liverpool University Press website as offering 'a new approach to the writing of literary history' not organised according to nation states but by transnational region. 'American Tropics' therefore refers to 'a kind of extended Caribbean', an imaginative space which offers 'a differently-centred literary history from those conventionally produced as US, Caribbean, or Latin American literature' (Liverpool University Press website). Also focusing on a geographical angle to literary history, Martin Brückner and Hsuan Hsu's edited collection *American Literary Geographies: Spatial Practice and Cultural Production, 1500–1900* (2007) uses the plural term to signal the various ways in which the essays included in their book explore 'intersections between geography and American literary history', contributing to literary history by 'emphasizing spatial over temporal frameworks as organizing principles or telling the story of American literature' (University of Delaware Press website), an explanation which makes clear the literary aims of the book.

(III) LITERARY GEOGRAPHY AND DISTANT READING

An entirely different definition of literary geography as method in literary studies was established in comparative literature in the late 1990s with the publication of Franco Moretti's *Atlas of the European Novel* (1998). Focusing on 'distant' (data-driven) analysis as opposed to close reading, and employing a diagrammatic form of mapping, Moretti also called his approach 'literary geography':

> [Y]ou select a textual feature ... find the data, put them on paper – and then you look at the map. In the hope that the visual construct will be more than the sum of its parts: that it will show a shape, a pattern ... this is what literary geography is all about.
>
> (Moretti, 1998: 13)

Although there has been some integration, or at least exchange of ideas, between Moretti's data-based graphic approach and the contemporary interdiscipline of literary geography, his line of work was not originally connected to either academic geography or cartographic theory.

(IV) THE READER'S LITERARY GEOGRAPHY

In his *New Critical Idiom* volume on *Spatiality* (2013) Robert J. Tally Jr. proposed yet another literary geography – 'the reader's literary geography' – in which a 'critical reader becomes a kind of geographer who actively interprets the literary map in such a way as to present new, sometimes hitherto unforeseen mappings' (2013: 78). In Tally's explanation here 'literary map' refers to the way in which 'writers map the real and imagined spaces of their world in various ways through literary means', which means that in this version of literary cartography and literary geography a reader's 'hitherto unforeseen mappings' are not literal maps but new textual readings. While Tally acknowledged that 'literary geography also refers to a field of study, and there are a number of scholars actively engaged in it', he explained that when he uses the term he means 'something a little broader and perhaps more metaphorical' (79–80).

CRITICAL LITERARY GEOGRAPHY, GEOCRITICISM AND SPATIAL LITERARY STUDIES

In addition to these various definitions of literary geography proposed since the beginning of the 1990s, several other new fields associated with spatial approaches to literary texts have been established. In 'The idea of a critical literary geography' (2005), literary critic Andrew Thacker took up the work on literature, space and place that had begun to emerge in literary studies in the 1990s to propose a fresh approach for literary criticism. Thacker called this new methodology 'critical literary geography' not to differentiate it from existing work within human geography (which he doesn't mention) but rather to distinguish it from the 'effortless mapping of represented landscapes in literary texts' which in his view characterised the popular (uncritical) literary geography of gazetteers and works of literary tourism. Thacker's critical literary geography involved the 'process of reading and interpreting literary texts by reference to geographical concepts such as space and place, social space, time-space compression, and spatial history' (60). Although what he proposed sounds quite similar to work being done at the time in the literary geography practised by human geographers, Thacker made it clear that he was 'primarily interested here in how far, and in what ways, the analysis of literary texts can be enriched by the use of geographical ideas and practices' (56). In other words, he located 'critical literary geography' within literary studies, and identified its primary aim as the analysis of literary texts. As an explicitly literary studies practice, critical literary geography is free from the responsibility to engage in detail with human geography theory and practice and the historiography of academic literary geography which distinguishes literary geography. Similar in many ways to Thacker's critical literary geography, and developed over the same time period, Robert J. Tally's version of geocriticism and the closely related project of spatial literary studies are also both primarily subfields in literary studies which promote spatially-inflected ways of reading and interpreting literary texts, again without requiring any in-depth understanding of work in academic geography. The distinction between these two literary projects and the mixed literary/geographical aims of literary geography can be understood most easily by considering first how work identifies its own aims and disciplinary context, and after that by assessing its level of interest in and knowledge of contemporary human geography.

WHAT IS THE 'GEOGRAPHY' IN LITERARY GEOGRAPHY?

One of the difficulties for non-geographers interested in understanding what literary geography is, what it can do and how it differs from literary studies, is that the commonplace, non-specialist definition of 'geography' is so different from the way in which the term is used and understood by contemporary human geographers. Robert Tally, for example, distinguishes spatial literary studies from literary geography on the basis of the idea that 'the significance of the word *spatial* is, of course, broader than that of *geographical*' and that, as a result, 'spatial criticism may just as easily deal with architecture as geography' (2020). For a human geographer working today, the idea that the 'spatial' and the 'geographical' can be separated and that 'spatial' is a broader term than 'geographical' would be puzzling, not least because so much work on spatial theory has been produced by geographers working within human geography: the influential 2005 monograph *For Space*, for example, was written, as geography, by geographer Doreen Massey. While acknowledging that some books in the *Geocriticism and Spatial Literary Studies* series 'have engaged more directly with geography and geographers', Tally lists three others in support of the idea that the 'spatial' extends beyond the geographical: one on cosmopolitanism, one on women and domestic space, and one on weird or fantastic spaces (Tally, 2020). All three of these topics have been the subjects of extensive work in contemporary human geography. The entry on 'cosmopolitanism' for the 2009 *International Encyclopedia of Human Geography*, for example, defines it as 'a broad-ranging term in sociopolitical and moral philosophy, which has been much debated in human geography'. Alison Blunt's 2005 review article for *Progress In Human Geography* on 'Cultural Geographies of Home' starts by looking back to Mona Domosh's 1998 review for the same journal, 'Geography and gender: home, again?' which deals with 'feminist geographical work on house and home, the household, and the domestic world'. Finally, 'weird or fantastic spaces' are another area of continuing interest for human geographers, and the chapter on literary 'weird geographies' included in the 2019 collection cited by Tally, *Spaces and Fictions of the Weird and Fantastic*, was contributed by geographer James Kneale as part of his work on literary geography, science fiction, horror and the fantastic. The kind of misunderstanding at work here which results from differing discipline-specific definitions of concepts and terms such as 'spatial' and 'geographical' is one of the main reasons why this book tries to clarify what 'geography' means for literary geographers, and what kind of work with literary texts, and collaborations with scholars working in other disciplines, their academic geography enables.

LITERARY GEOGRAPHY IN THE 21ST CENTURY

The active interdisciplinarity of literary geography began to increase significantly after the mid-1990s and early 2000s, as interest in space, place, mapping and geography in general began its rapid expansion in literary studies. While this interest was newly inspired by work in cultural studies, geography and spatial theory, in the context of the US academy it can also be retrospectively connected to sporadic instances of work on setting, place and geography in literary studies and also to the study of landscape, literature, and historical geography characteristic of the early years of interdisciplinary American Studies. In the UK, the trend toward spatial themes within literary studies built on earlier work which had dealt with topics such as the rural and the urban, the links connecting 18th-century landscape gardening, poetry and painting, and the interaction of the imagined and the actual in literary fiction. The trend toward geographical themes in UK-based literary criticism was significantly advanced by Thacker's 2005 article proposing critical literary geography as a new approach for literary criticism.

The early phases of this turn toward spatial themes in literary studies were generally achieved without reference to the human geography tradition of literary geography, although geographers had been benefiting from work in literary studies and promoting literary studies/literary geography collaborations for some time. This gap meant that until relatively recently, literary geographers were able to assume that their audience was made up almost entirely of human geographers. Perhaps as a result, they have been slow to provide colleagues in literary studies and other related disciplines with detailed explanations of the geographical roots of the interdiscipline. This has probably led to an assumption within literary studies that 'the cultural turn' in the humanities and social sciences was the key factor in what they took to be literary geography's recent 'emergence'.

Viewing the history of literary geography from a literary studies perspective, for example, Neal Alexander has dated the beginnings of academic literary geography only as far back as the 1980s and 90s, emphasising the idea that it was at that point that 'two distinct but related intellectual currents' (the spatial turn and the cultural turn) came together. Describing literary geography as 'one of the more striking manifestations of the ongoing spatial turn in the arts and humanities', Alexander suggests that it might also be regarded as a 'specific articulation of the cultural turn in human geography' (2015a: 14). Within geography as a whole, however, the cultural turn has not been associated particularly strongly with work on literary texts, and within literary geography it features as just one of the many theoretical and methodological turns which have been significant in its extended development. The landmark collection *Cultural Turns/Geographical Turns* (2000), for example, includes only one chapter by a literary geographer among its explorations of topics as diverse as culinary authenticity, workplace cultures and equal opportunities policies, Long-Term Capital Management, social policy, and the sense of touch (Cook et al., 2000).

The 2012 launch of an online interdisciplinary bibliography for work across the range of plural literary geographies was one of various relatively recent attempts to establish an active interdisciplinary collaboration able to bridge these disciplinary gaps. The launch of the open-access online interdisciplinary journal *Literary Geographies* a few years later subsequently provided the field with a venue for publication which was not discipline-specific. Nevertheless, although individual examples of fused literary/geographical work can be traced back at least to the 1940s, and some literary geographers continue to produce work useful and connected to both contributing disciplines, the interdisciplinarity of the central core of literary geography still faces some significant challenges.

(I) DISCONNECTIONS

In the late 1990s/early 2000s, when an interest in spatial themes was first becoming established within literary studies, literary critics were mostly unaware that there was a longstanding 'geography and literature' subfield in the social science/humanities framework of human geography. As a result, work in the early years of interest in spatial and geographical themes within literary studies was generally disconnected from parallel ongoing work in human geography. Before the turn of the 21st century geographers worked with literary texts and referred to work in literary studies primarily in the pursuit and practice of geographical aims and methods. In academic literary studies, however, an intermittent interest in space, place, landscape and mapping had yet to gain traction as a major initiative, and there was very little contact with, or even awareness of, literary geography as a subfield in human geography. As a result, until very recently, geographers working with literary texts tended to take it for granted that their work would be of little interest to literary critics. Part of the reason for this was that the kind of geography which was influential in literary studies in the first stages of the turn toward spatial themes was not literary geography but the more general spatial theory of geographers such as David Harvey and Edward Soja, sociologists such as Henri Lefebevre and critical cartographers such as Brian Harley.

(II) DIFFERENCES

When literary studies was first developing its broad interest in spatial themes there was very little exploration of the potential of an interdisciplinary collaboration with existing geographical work on literature, despite considerable interest in spatial theory and cultural geography more generally. Then, even when it became evident that there was the potential to merge, or at least connect, compatible work in literary studies and human geography, the difficulties that would have to be negotiated in order to bring such a collaboration into effect were not fully grasped. This was for two connected reasons: first, it was assumed that what appeared to be a mutual research focus and a shared set of terms would be enough to enable collaboration; and second, the extent of the differences in aims and methods which characterised the two fields was routinely underestimated. In retrospect, the essence of the problem might be explained in rather obvious and reductive terms with the proposal that the focus of literary studies is literature, while in human geography it is geography. Phrased differently, where literary studies has conventionally been held together by its interest in a shared subject matter (literary texts), the coherence of contemporary human geography is more likely to be based on a shared way of thinking, an approach, an academic lens which can be applied to any given subject matter (literature, art, surfing, walking, museums, housework ...). So we could say that, for literary studies, literary geography is one of many possible angles of approach to a shared and central object of study, while, for human geography, literary geography is more like the application of a shared and central approach to one of many possible objects of study.

(III) COLLABORATION

Ideally, of course, work in literary geography would contribute to both literary studies and human geography, and there are certainly many possible connections and shared interests on which to build. But the collaborative partnership which could flourish within literary geographies can only be achieved by acknowledging and working with disparities in historiographies, aims and methods, not by ignoring or flattening them out. Full consensus on the definition and purpose of literary geography is unlikely, not least because the interdiscipline in some cases extends beyond literary studies and human geography: literary cartography, for example, at present not only connects literary studies and human geography but also, in many cases, cartography and cartographic software tools (known as GIS, or geographic information systems). However, while it might seem discouraging to acknowledge that the integration of literary geography cannot be achieved in any straightforward way, simply on the basis of a shared interest in literature and geography, it is probably sufficient progress for the time being to be aware of the obstacles raised by these differences. This recognition of difference is the necessary first step towards the negotiation of ways forward.

How is it possible to generate a sustainably collaborative literary geography? The proposal offered here, perhaps paradoxically, is to resist any attempt to impose and defend a specific definition or set of aims and practices, the idea being that any strong move in that direction is more likely to generate an atomisation of the field than to achieve consensus. On the other hand, an awareness and acceptance of variations in practice may avoid such a breakdown. In order to understand the assumptions about aims, methods, and the definition of 'sophistication' stitched into work in any given publication or presentation, and to make progress, we need to understand the discipline-specific framework(s) which informed the construction and expression of that work. This makes comparative historiography and a sensitivity to the varying implications of apparently common terminology essential for the future of an integrated literary geography.

ACADEMIC AND POPULAR LITERARY GEOGRAPHY

Before the 1980s, there were two main forms of literary geography. One – academic literary geography – started out as a subfield of human geography, appearing most commonly as scholarly articles in geography journals. This line of work, which began in the late 19th century and developed steadily after the 1920s, eventually became known by the term 'literary geography' in the 1970s. The other main form of literary geography existing before the 1980s was aimed at the general reader and consisted primarily of mass-market literary gazetteers and guides for tourists. William Sharp's *Literary Geography* of 1904, an early example of this genre, was intended to be 'a readable companion in times of leisure' (Sharp, 1904: foreword). This early tradition of popular literary geography was sustained through the late 20th century with works such as Margaret Drabble and Jorge Lewinski's *A Writer's Britain: Landscape in Literature* (1979), and David Daiches and John Flower's *Literary Landscapes of the British Isles: A Narrative Atlas* (1979).

The fact that early literary geography took these two distinct forms has led to some confusion about its origins, with literary critics tending to associate the beginnings of literary geography with popular gazetteers and works of literary tourism, and geographers identifying the foundations of the field as academic work within human geography. As a result, literary scholars have located the beginnings of the field in non-academic publications aimed at the general public, such as Sharp's *Literary Geography*, with its chapters on 'Thackeray-land' and 'The Country of George Eliot', in which the author hopes his readers will 'share his own pleasure in wandering through these "literary lands"' (Sharp, 1904: foreword). Geographers, meanwhile, have tended to locate the origins of literary geography in

INTRODUCTION 15

early academic or classroom-oriented work in human geography, often starting with the geologist Archibald Geikie's 1898 *Types of Scenery and Their Influence on Literature*. Other notable early work in the geographical tradition include H.R. Mill's 1910 chapter on 'Geography in Literature' in his *Guide to Geographical Books and Appliances* and J.K. Wright's series of essays for the *Geographical Review* in the 1920s. Considerable confusion has arisen from the fact that literary critics tend to focus on the earliest use of the term 'literary geography', while geographers have concentrated on the earliest appearance of academic work on geography and literary texts, to which the term 'literary geography' was applied within geography well after the subfield had been established under titles such as 'landscape in literature' or 'literature and geography'.

LITERARY GEOGRAPHY IN LITERARY STUDIES

The term 'literary geography' was rarely used by literary critics before the late 1990s. A very early exception was Virginia Woolf's 1905 *Times Literary Supplement* review of *The Thackeray Country* and *The Dickens Country*, in which she made several critically prescient points in discussing works of popular literary geography. Donald Heiney's 'Illiers and Combray: a study in literary geography' (1955), which appeared in *Twentieth Century Literature*, is another very rare exception, seemingly coming out of nowhere and generating only a very few subsequent citations. Heiney argued that the interplay in Proust's writing between the historical Illiers and the fictional Combray was essential to Proust studies, a theme which should have connected with later work in literary geography but apparently didn't. Work in literary studies that would in time become significant for literary geography (despite not being so labelled) from the early to mid-20th century includes M.M. Bakhtin's argument for the connectedness of literary time and space in his 1937 essay 'Forms of time and of the chronotope in the novel' and Joseph Frank's introduction of the concept of spatial form in his 1945 two-part essay on spatial form in modern literature. Where Bakhtin was interested in how distinctive literary space-time configurations shaped and characterised particular genres, such as 19th-century French realism, Frank drew attention to the non-linear structure of literary works in which the narrative is distributed spatially throughout the text.

THE NEW CULTURAL GEOGRAPHY

In the 1990s and early 2000s, the human geography variant of literary geography experienced a period of regeneration corresponding with the rise of what was known at the time as the 'new cultural geography'. The 'newness' of this form of cultural geography lies in the ways in which the largely UK-based initiative broke from an earlier US-based form of cultural geography, developed in the 1920s by Carl Sauer at UCLA Berkeley. Sauerian cultural geography focused on distinctive areas 'fashioned from a natural landscape by a cultural group', with the natural area providing the medium, and the local way of life (culture) providing the agent, the result being 'the cultural landscape'. In contrast, the 'new cultural geography' focused on how 'cultural differences comprise the human world'.

> The sense in which ... the human world is not distinct from (or at least not independent of) its *representations* – became a mainstream concern: culture was constitutive, performative, always-already in the making. Despite some outstanding debts to the Berkeley School of cultural geography – notably an abiding interest in landscape – the new cultural geography owed more to the growth of cultural studies.
>
> (Clarke, 2017: online)

THE CULTURAL TURN

Although the 'new' cultural geography has sometimes been conflated with a wider 'cultural turn' which took place in the humanities and social sciences between the 1970s and the 2000s, the 'cultural turn' names a much broader shift in subjects and priorities across the humanities and the social sciences. Broadly speaking, while the cultural turn drew on the work of a wide range of thinkers and theories, it was articulated in the form most significant for geography in the work of Stuart Hall, Paul Gilroy and others at the University of Birmingham's Centre for Contemporary Cultural Studies (UK). The impact of the cultural turn in geography was arguably most influential not on the development of literary geography or even cultural geography in general but in fields such as economic geography and critical geopolitics (Rosati, 2017: online).

THE SPATIAL TURN

At the same time that the 'new cultural geography' was being established in the social sciences, an increased interest in space and place in the humanities – sometimes called the 'spatial turn' – led to the emergence of a line of spatially-oriented work in literary studies. Leonard Lutwack's *The Role of Place in Literature*, for example, which appeared in 1984, referred to 'a new interest in place both as a formal element in literature' and 'as an important issue in general', resulting from a new 'public recognition that earth as a place, or the total environment is being radically changed and perhaps rendered uninhabitable' (2). Lutwack in this way foreshadowed the emergence of ecocriticism and geopoetics, while also having a direct influence on D.C.D. Pocock's work on literary geography in the UK: he is cited six times in Pocock's 1988 review article on geography and literature for *Progress in Human Geography*, in which Pocock mentions that although Lutwack's work was one of a few hopeful exceptions, in general the literary studies/human geography 'interface' had been 'largely unidirectional' (Pocock, 1988: 87).

CHALLENGES FACING INTERDISCIPLINARY COLLABORATION

The first decade of the 21st century was an era of some uncertainty in literary geography as well as in thematically related fields in literary studies, because of a lack of clarity or overview regarding the disciplinary identity of work engaging with literature and spatial theory, and the ways in which various fields were connected or disconnected by aims, methods and terminologies. As the confusion begins to clear we now have a much better understanding of how these various fields are linked and how they differ. Critical literary geography, geocriticism and spatial literary studies remain primarily subfields of literary studies, and while they have all benefited from the widely disseminated ideas of spatial theorists such as David Harvey and Henri Lefebvre, they rarely draw on the long history of the 'literature and geography' tradition in human geography. In contrast, a major aim of contemporary literary geography is to nurture an explicit collaboration between geographers and literary studies scholars which is able to take into account the aims and methods of both fields. The simplest way to distinguish literary geography from related work in literary studies is to consider the extent to which its historiographical and disciplinary context includes geographical as well as literary work with texts. In contemporary literary geography, aims and methods from both disciplinary traditions would ideally work in partnership.

(I) RECOGNISING DIFFERENCES

The biggest problem currently inhibiting the development of a fully merged collaborative literary geography is (paradoxically) that the differences in aims and methods it has to contain are frequently underestimated, for reasons outlined earlier. Traditionally, for geographers, the term 'literary geography' has described a subfield of human geography, with the 'literary' describing the direction in which geographical method is being applied. In academic literary studies, on the other hand, the term 'literary geography' has been more likely to describe one angle of approach to a central and assumed subject matter.

(II) RESPECT

A second issue inhibiting the establishment of a collaborative core for literary geography is the difficulty of recognising what constitutes useful or mature work in different disciplines and, as a result, what can be accepted as good practice in literary geography. Assumptions about the definition of developed thinking naturally vary according to discipline, which is one of the reasons why literary critics have sometimes been rather disparaging of the level of academic sophistication to be found in the kind of literary geography practiced within human geography. Of course, until the early 21st century, literary geography was mostly produced by scholars intending to write human geography, not literary criticism. When the standard is assumed to be 'sophisticated reading' rather than 'sophisticated geography', work intended to generate progress in human geography, as opposed to advances in critical practice, can seem clumsy to literary critics. This lack of confidence in the academic refinement of literary geography has at times, paradoxically, been encouraged by dismissive critiques of the subfield made by mainstream human geographers.

(III) FAMILIARITY AND ACCESSIBILITY

A third complication inhibiting interdisciplinary collaboration has been unfamiliarity with, or limited access to, relevant publications and conference presentations in different academic traditions. For example, work in literary criticism and in human geography has traditionally been published in single-discipline journals and publisher categories, and as a result it has been difficult for any one reader to be aware of innovation in both areas. Work presented in conferences is even harder to access. Adding to these access problems is the complication that literary geography has a broad international historiography and there is undoubtedly much useful work published outside the US/UK mainstream, sometimes in English and more often in other languages. Recent developments in search engine technology have made it possible to recuperate some of this work and retrospectively integrate it into the history of literary geography, but much of it remains unknown. An important part of the rationale behind the launch of the journal *Literary Geographies* was the need to create a venue for publication which did not presuppose a specifically literary or geographical audience, and which would be accessible to authors and readers without institutional access to expensive anglophone 'international' journals. Not surprisingly, both the peer-review process and the copy-editing stage tend to turn up difficulties in interdisciplinary communication, particularly when an author is using terms and concepts with obvious connotations in their own field or native language but which do not function in the same way for readers trained in a different field or situated in a different institutional system.

(IV) TERMINOLOGY

This communication problem reveals clearly how the use of apparently shared but in fact divisive terminology has created a fourth significant barrier to literary geography. Attempts to create a literary geography able to generate work which draws from and contributes to both literary studies and human geography has revealed the problematic communication gap caused when identical terms mean radically different things in different disciplinary contexts. There is also the general problem that while spatial terms tend to be taken literally in human geography they are often used metaphorically in literary studies; for geographers the issue here, as explained by Neil Smith and Cindi Katz, is that 'spatial metaphors are problematic in so far as they presume that space is not' (1993: 73). Mapping, cognitive mapping, critical literary geography and literary cartography are all terms which are used quite differently and carry very different connotations in literary studies and in human geography. This would be less of a challenge if there were greater mutual recognition of the differences and how they inhibit cross-disciplinary communication, but at least at present (for the reasons outlined earlier) such an understanding is not commonplace.

WAYS FORWARD

Incompatible terminologies can be dealt with once the differences are recognised and understood. Unfamiliarity with material produced by the 'other side' participating in literary geography can be overcome with effort, increased communication and explicitly interdisciplinary bibliographies and publication venues. The final issue has to do with the fundamental need to respect the aims and methods of other disciplines and to be ready to step outside a discipline-specific understanding of literary geography. This relates to what is probably the major issue facing the negotiation of interdisciplinarity in contemporary literary geography: what (precisely) is its subject matter and what (exactly) does it do?

While literary geography continues to embrace a variety of techniques, aims and methods, some more literary and others more geographical, it remains distinct from kindred fields in literary studies such as geocriticism and spatial literary studies, most obviously because of its continuing active engagement with the aims, practices and history of human geography. The coherence and interdisciplinarity of literary geography depends on the way in which it brings together not only literary texts and lived geographies but also theory and practice in academic literary studies and human geography. In addition, literary geography is becoming an increasingly distinctive and coherent interdiscipline as its specialists not only create a shared theoretical vocabulary but also generate a 'literary geography context' for writing in the field, by showing how new work connects to its historiography. The distinctive interdisciplinarity of literary geography is already being articulated in the citation practices, which characteristically refer not only to (1) primary literary texts and the geography of the lived world, as well as (2) work in literary studies and in human geography and spatial theory, but also (3) to a growing framework of interdisciplinary theory and practice specific to literary geography. An appreciation for the deep historiography and broad current practice of literary geography is essential to pre-empt the idea that literary geography is a 'nascent' or 'emergent' field, 'towards' the establishment of which we need to be working. This is not to say, of course, that literary geographers anticipate any kind of arrival at a final destination: they have been travelling hopefully for more than a century now, and expect to keep going.

OVERVIEW OF THIS BOOK

The purpose of this book is to provide readers with an introduction to literary geography which will enable them to make sense of the ways in which the interdiscipline is practiced today.

Readers will become able to recognise what kind of assumptions are embedded in its various traditions, appreciate where those assumptions come from, and understand why individual projects within literary geography can sometimes seem disconnected. The book is intended to contribute to the retrospective construction of an integrated comparative historiography and an overview of present practice which will function as a platform for future interdisciplinary work and collaboration at the 'literary geography' centre of the broader range of plural 'literary geographies'. The book can be divided into two main sections: the first reviews the various historiographical lines now coming together in contemporary literary geography, discusses its aims and methods, and outlines the range of literary genres and themes covered by work in the field so far. The second section takes up two key themes which have been particularly significant in literary geography, mappings and representation, before turning to a speculative consideration of how literary geography might develop in the near future. The book ends with a chapter providing compact definitions of key terms and concepts.

1

ORIGINS

In the late 1990s, as literary critics began to read spatial theory, and geographers engaged with questions of representation and textuality, opportunities for interdisciplinary exchange of ideas and methods between literary studies and the geographical subfield of literary geography increased. Those opportunities created the potential for a more actively interdisciplinary literary geography, which could have emerged had there been a better mutual understanding at the time of the differences separating the histories, aims, methods and key terms of literary studies and human geography. Unfortunately, as suggested by the fact that literary geography is, even today, routinely described by non-geographers as an 'emerging' body of work, literary critics remained generally unaware of, or uninterested in, literary geography as an expression of human geography's engagement with literary texts. The opportunity which had opened up in the 1990s for an actively interdisciplinary literary geography was for the time being lost. Several decades later, with new opportunities for cooperation, there is now a second chance to attempt a literary geography able to negotiate the historical divisions which separate work in literary studies from work in human geography. The realisation of an actively collaborative interdiscipline now depends on the reciprocal development of a greater awareness not only of how the two fields work separately but also how they could work together.

TWO REVIEW ESSAYS, 1994 AND 1998

A comparison of two articles from the 1990s reveals the distance separating literary geography from literary studies at that time: the first, Marc Brosseau's 'Geography's literature', was published in *Progress in Human Geography* in 1994; the second, John Kerrigan's 'The country of the mind: exploring the links between geography and the writer's imagination', was published in the *Times Literary Supplement* in 1998. While one is very much in the human geography mode and the other a contribution to literary criticism, they deal with recognisably similar topics and have both been influential, with Brosseau's making its impact in human geography, and Kerrigan's in literary studies. Since publication, Brosseau's article has been extensively cited by geographers, but has achieved very little recognition among literary critics; it is only in the past few years that it has started to be cited beyond books and articles written by geographers for geographers. Similarly, but in reverse, Kerrigan's article went unremarked by geographers, but had a significant impact on the literary studies version of literary geography launched by Andrew Thacker in his influential 2005 article, 'The idea of a critical literary geography'. Thacker cited Kerrigan's thoughts on 'how valuable the findings of a new literary geography could be' (Kerrigan, 1998: 4) in proposing a literary geography for literary critics that would be able to respond to the fact that 'since the early 1990s ... questions of space and geography have become recognised as legitimate and important topics in many areas of literary and cultural studies' (57–58). Because Kerrigan's view of the 'old' literary geography was that it had been a false start in humanistic geography which had quickly fizzled out, Thacker had no encouragement to make the connection between his proposed 'critical literary geography' and existing literary geography, as practised mainly (but not entirely) by human geographers.

The Brosseau and Kerrigan articles differ markedly in their orientation toward work outside their own field. In proposing 'a much greater focus on the text itself' (349) Brosseau was responding to the greater emphasis on discourse and textuality which had developed in human geography as a whole by the mid-1990s, and encouraging geographers to incorporate more work from literary criticism. He asked literary geographers to respect the geographical significance of literary style and narrative method, and to treat literary text as a 'complex signifying practice' (349). In a 1995 review essay on landscape geography for *Progress in Human Geography*, James Duncan reported that the study of literature in geography was 'being taken to a new level' by a group of scholars, including Marc Brosseau, who had 'a view of the humanities which is critical, tough minded and very much *au courant de* debates within literary and cultural theory' (419). Joanne Sharp, for example, 'shows that literature not only can force readers to grapple with questions of cultural identity and alterity but can also be an active force in political and cultural "geo-graphing" of the world outside the text' (419).

Writing four years after Brosseau, Kerrigan's essay also emphasised the value of collaboration between literary critics and geographers, but because he based his vision of a 'new' literary geography on a radically simplified version of the history of human geography, which erased almost all of its engagement with literary texts (including the Brosseau and Sharp articles from 1994 to 1996), he eliminated much of the historiography most relevant to his vision. Presenting the future of literary geography as a geographically-informed approach within literary criticism, Kerrigan's intervention meant that for literary studies one of the paradoxical effects of the increased interest in spatial themes, which had motivated his essay, was the establishment of the idea that literary geography was either a limited and ultimately failed experiment by humanistic geographers or a form of popular literary tourism, 'the sort of guide which belongs in the glove compartment of a car' (Kerrigan, 1998: 4).

20TH CENTURY ACADEMIC LITERARY GEOGRAPHY: TWO VERSIONS

The 'sort of guide' to which Kerrigan was referring falls into the category of popular literary gazetteers or books for literary tourists, one of the two originating forms of literary geography. While these double origins are now generally acknowledged, in 1990 geographers Allan Noble and Ramesh Dhussa still associated the term 'literary geography' solely with academic work in human geography, regarding William Sharp's *Literary Geography* – an early example of the popular form – as 'not a work in literary geography' at all (1990: 50). Noble and Dhussa's review of literary geography for *Journal of Cultural Geography* covered the period from 1910 to the late 1980s, by which time, in their view, 'literary geography seemed to be well established as a recognized research specialization of the larger [geographical] discipline' (59). Noting that the number of papers on literary geography at the annual meeting of the Association of American Geographers remained 'small but constant', they considered the possibility that a 'plateau of interest' had been reached. They contemplated two possibilities for post-1990 literary geography: the more pessimistic was that 'the subject has been exhausted as a source of intellectual inquiry'; the alternative was that

> initial directions have been pursued and original objectives reached and that a kind of marking time is occurring during which materials will be digested and gains in scholarship consolidated until a new spurt of creative energy is released, perhaps by an as yet unrecognized scholar.
>
> (61)

Four years after Noble and Dhussa's review, the publication of Marc Brosseau's 'Geography's literature' in *Progress in Human Geography*, based on his recently completed PhD thesis, indicated that the more hopeful of the two possible futures was being realised.

Nevertheless, in his 1998 sketch of the history of human geography in 'The country of the mind', John Kerrigan disregarded the history of geographical work with literary texts sketched by Noble and Dhussa. Not surprisingly, this had a negative impact on the awareness and understanding of literary geography within literary studies. Presenting the emergence of humanistic literary geography in the 1970s as something entirely new, a reaction to 'the waves of grand theory and quantitative analysis which swept through the subject in the 1960s' (3), Kerrigan's version of human geography was able to overlook its sustained interest in literary texts for a couple of reasons: first, he concentrated on mainstream interests; and second, he focused on monographs or book-length collections. For much of its history, however, the geographical subfield of work with literary texts was sustained not in book publications but in articles published in geographical journals and in presentations and discussions at conferences; book-length studies only began to appear in the 1970s. In fact all of the examples Kerrigan provides of what happened when 'adventurous geographers turned to literature' are taken from one edited collection: D.C.D. Pocock's 1981 *Humanistic Geography and Literature*, which, by the time of his review essay, was some 17 years old. According to Kerrigan, as geographers in the 1970s began to reconsider 'the importance of agency and affect in the shaping and use of space' it 'did not long escape them that a great deal of poetry and prose fiction ... is about how people belong to places or are alienated from them, how they reimagine their surroundings and infuse localities with emotion' (3). In other words, Kerrigan suggests that it was a revelation to geographers in the 1970s that poetry and prose fiction could be used as a resource in the study of people's relationships with places and localities.

J.K. WRIGHT

Although Kerrigan's understanding was that geographical work with literary texts had been a new development in the 1970s, Noble and Dhussa had noted in their 1990 review essay that 'as early as the 1920s, a few American geographers began to express the view that literary works could be explored to understand more fully the meaning of both natural and cultural worlds' (52). Two major American geographers of this era, Carl Sauer and

John Kirtland Wright, 'realised independently ... that literature was an untapped resource which opened up an altogether new dimension in understanding space' (52). While Sauer 'drew the attention of future researchers toward literature' in a general sense, J.K. Wright had a direct impact on the beginnings of academic literary geography. Wright's legacy in geographical perception, humanistic geography, geographical subjectivity and literary geography is reviewed in Michael Handley's 'John K. Wright and human nature in geography' (1993). Handley explains that although by the early 20th century human geography in general was prioritising environmental determinism, Sauer's 'Foreword to historical geography' (1941) was an early 'recognition of the importance of perception in geography'. Handley also makes the point that where Sauer was interested in the geographical knowledge of elites and of cultures as entireties, Wright's interest was in 'all levels of geographical thinking', his new term 'geosophy' referring to 'the study of geographical knowledge from any or all points of view'. Wright's ideas resurfaced in the early 1960s with the publication of David Lowenthal's 'Geography, Experience, and Imagination' (1961), which would form the basis for later studies in subjective and imaginative geographies.

Similarly, although it was Kerrigan's understanding that the modern development of geography 'involved a calculated detachment from the literary', J.K. Wright's influence on literary geography began with a series of unsigned essays for the *Geographical Review* in the 1920s and 1930s, which looked in turn at 'Geography in literature', 'The geography of Dante', 'Homeric geography', 'Geography of the Odyssey' and 'Bibliographical sources for geographical fiction'. And while Kerrigan claimed that perhaps the earliest example of a form of literary geography, Strabo's discussion of Homer in his 'Geography', 'has been of little interest to geographers since the eighteenth century', one of Wright's early essays, 'A plea for the history of geography' (1926) opens with a discussion of Strabo's debates with Erasthenes on the question of whether Homer should be read as a poet or a scientific authority. Taken as a whole, Wright's publications in this era provide evidence of the early years of a tradition of geographical work with literary texts. While there is some legitimacy to Kerrigan's view that while the 'commanding founders of the discipline' were skilled writers, the 'positivism which drove their subject discouraged reflexive thinking about linguistic aspects of culture', Wright's essays, along with other work in literary geography from the 1910s to 1930s, show that this is an oversimplification.

In the long run, J.K. Wright's primary influence on literary geography is likely to have stemmed not so much from his essays for *Geographical Review* as from his Presidential address to the 1946 meeting of the American Association of Geographers, subsequently published in the association's Annals as 'Terrae incognitae: the place of the imagination in geography' (1947). Here Wright restated his lifelong interest in the geographical ideas 'of all manner of people – not only geographers, but farmers and fishermen, business executives and poets, novelists and painters' (1947: 12). It was this interest in the geographical imagination ('geosophy') that made Wright's work, published between the mid-1920s and the late 1940s, so important for literary geography. While it is true that Wright was always somewhat out of step with the dominant aims and methods of American geography during his lifetime, his long-term contribution to human geography in general, and literary geography in particular, turned out to be of major significance. Wright's importance for the history of literary geography rests on two points: first, the emphasis he placed on the geographical imagination and subjectivity in geographical research; and second his openness to the value of literary sources.

ACADEMIC LITERARY GEOGRAPHY 1910–1940

While Strabo's *Geography* and Von Humboldt's *Cosmos* of 1847, two works dealing with geography and art, are sometimes cited as the starting points for modern literary geography, geographical work with literary texts has more commonly been dated from Scottish geologist Archibald Geikie's 1898 *Types of Scenery and Their Influence on Literature*. First presented as the 1898 annual public lecture at Oxford University and published in the same year, *Types of Scenery* sets out to 'discuss the leading types of scenery that distinguish the British Isles, and to inquire how far it may be possible to trace from each of them an influence upon the growth of English literature' (6). Noble and Dhussa give an alternative starting point for literary geography in their 1990 review essay, dating its history from climatologist H.R. Mill's 1910 *Guide to Geographical Books and Appliances*, citing specifically its chapter on 'Geographical novels', which for them marked 'the first serious consideration of the value and use of literature by a geographer' (51).

Mill's *Guide* of 1910 was also mentioned by Wright in his 1924 essay 'Geography in literature'. While Wright notes that Mill provides accurate and lively descriptions useful for teaching purposes, for him the value of the geographical novels described by Mill goes beyond setting:

> [S]cenes are frequently described at some length, and, better still, they may form an integral part of the narrative, as when the peculiarities of the district or of the people influence the course of the story. This is an important part of the value of a geographical novel: it may show by actual examples that working out of the various forces and interaction of the various factors that is of the essence of geography
>
> (59)

Where Geikie was interested in the influence of types of scenery on the development of English literature, and Mill was concerned with lively description and the interactions of place and people, Elias Lieberman's *The American Short Story: A Study of the Influence of Locality in its Development* (1912) focused on the impact of local geography on literary production in the USA. A little later, in 1920, the Leeds Branch of the British Geographical Association published D. Wharton's *Short List of Novels and Literary Works of Geographic Interest*. Work on literary texts and geography published in the UK in this era also included J.N.L. Baker's article 'The geography of Daniel Defoe' for the *Scottish Geographical Journal* in 1931. Baker emphasises Defoe's 'great skill' in blending fact and fiction in the production of textual geography, despite the fact that he travelled very little and that as a result 'his knowledge came from wide reading, from diligent study of newspapers, and from contact with a great variety of men' (258). Baker's article marks a very early example of work dealing with the way fiction combines and blends 'real world' and 'imagined' geographies: not simply 'representing' landscapes and places but articulating a mixed geographical knowledge made up from different kinds of information and knowledge, some firsthand, some the result of reading and conversation.

J.K. Wright also mentions Robert Ramsay's 1921 *Short Stories of America*, which included 16 short stories 'illustrative of various ways in which local color may be depicted', along with a map dividing the US and Alaska into five major divisions and 25 'subordinate local color states' which Wright notes 'mark off one from another wholly independent regions each one characterized by a sufficiently individualistic type of life to have given rise to a distinctive type of story' (659). Wright concludes his 1924 review 'Geography in literature' with a paragraph on Septime Gorceix's 1923 *Le Miroir de la France: Géographie littéraire des grandes régions françaises*, which includes excerpts from novels, poems, essays and descriptions, 'chosen for the poignancy with which they depict the various pays and cities of France' (660). But where earlier works had primarily been books for the general reader, this was a scholarly article in the tradition of regional geography. French-language literary geography would return to the spotlight in English-language literary geography again in the 1990s, with Canadian geographer Marc Brosseau's Université Paris-Sorbonne PhD thesis 'Des romans-géographes: le roman et la connaissance géographique des lieux' (1992). Completed two years before his article 'Geography's literature', Brosseau's thesis proposes 'a dialogical approach which considers the novel as a subject and not merely an object under analysis' (1992). By 'subject' Brosseau means that the novel itself is capable of creating geography, that 'the literary text may constitute a geographer in its own right as it generates norms, particular models of readability, that produce a particular type of geography' (1994: 349). For Brosseau, thinking of the novel as a subject with agency enables the literary geographer to engage respectfully with the ways in which it articulates knowledge about human space and place.

LITERARY ORIGINS 1900–1970

William Sharp's *Literary Geography* of 1904 and Virginia Woolf's review essay 'Literary Geography', published in the *Times Literary Supplement* in 1905, are the two works most commonly cited within literary studies as marking the beginnings of literary geography. It is typically also remarked, however, that these early works were restricted to the basic practice of linking authors with places, landscapes, and regions. Moving quickly past Sharp's *Literary Geography* and Woolf's review, literary critics have tended to date the beginnings of properly 'critical' (academic) literary geography only as far back as the 1980s. Neal Alexander, for example, notes that while the gazetteer style of literary geography 'continues to manifest itself in the form of literary tourism ventures and coffee-table books', this rudimentary approach to literary geography 'has largely been superseded in an academic context by more sophisticated critical formulations' (2015a: 4). Reviewing the field from a literary perspective, he is using the term 'critical' here to refer to the practice of literary criticism, not critical geography.

While it is true that Sharp's *Literary Geography* might be regarded in this way, as one of Kerrigan's 'amiable books', Woolf's essay gives an early indication of more academic discussion, because while it deals with two conventional literary guidebooks – *The Thackeray Country* (1905) and *The Dickens Country* (1905) – the review itself moves beyond simple mapping to make the point that the fictional 'phantom cities' of Thackeray and Dickens should not be too easily linked to 'tangible brick and mortar'. In its insistence that the 'writer's country is a territory within his own brain', Woolf's 1905 review makes an early contribution to the still current debate about the relationship of literary space to the lived world. The review is, as a result, important not because of its subject matter but because it is an early example of commentary on the problematic conflation of literary and physical locations. As Andrew Thacker points out, 'Woolf's approach is more than simply a realist attempt to map certain locations within London; instead, it demonstrates a complex intertwining of material spaces with a thematics of power and an exploration of how geography and space shapes and informs human character' (2016: 411–412).

A third publication from the early 20th century which provided useful information on popular literary geography in this era is the *Bibliography of Literary Geography* (1918) prepared by Edith J. Roswell Hawley for the Library School of the New York Public Library at the time of her graduation. The first instalment of this bibliography appeared in 1915 in *The Bulletin of Bibliography* (available online at the Internet Archive), primarily listing articles in the New York Public Library but also including a few titles taken from the Library of Congress depository catalogue. Concentrating on well-known English and American authors, the lengthy bibliography, published over several years, lists gazetteers and works of literary tourism, 'armchair' and actual. William Henry Bideing's *In the Land of Lorna Doone and Other Pleasurable Excursions in England* [c.1895] is a typical entry, with the list of its contents including 'In Cornwall with an umbrella', and 'A bit of Yorkshire coast'.

Two mid-20th century works in literary studies that are important sources for literary geography are Mikhail Bakhtin's 'Forms of time and of the chronotope in the novel' (originally published 1937–1938) and Joseph Frank's 'Spatial form in modern literature' (1945). Bakhtin's understanding of the connectedness of literary time and space in his theory of the chronotope led to his argument that distinctive literary space–time configurations shaped and characterised particular genres, such as 19th-century French realism. Geographers were reading Bakhtin as a literary/spatial theorist in the early 2000s, with the 2000 collection *Thinking Space* including a chapter on Bakhtin by Julian Holloway and James Kneale: 'Mikhail Bakhtin: dialogics of space'.

A few years after Bakhtin published his essay on the chronotope, Joseph Frank drew attention to the non-linear structure of literary works, specifically the ways in which narrative is distributed spatially throughout the text. Marc Brosseau demonstrates the significance of both Frank and Bakhtin for literary geography in his 1995 discussion of John Dos Passos's novel *Manhattan Transfer*. According to Brosseau, because the novel 'develops time and space interactions that match the pace and fragmentation of modern urban life', its 'chronology can only be reconstituted through a somewhat artificial process' (95). This 'staccato treatment of time, whereby events follow one another without clear transition nor relative chronological ordering during the reading experience, suggests the frantic pace of life' in the New York brought to life by the narrative (96). As Brosseau points out, this particular chronotope has some similarities with Frank's idea of spatial form. Talking of Pound, Proust and Joyce, Frank argues that all three 'ideally intend the reader to apprehend their work spatially, in a moment of time, rather than as a sequence' (Frank, quoted in Brosseau, 1995: 96). Brosseau notes that although the events in *Ulysses* all happen within a single day, those of *Manhattan Transfer* unfold over a period of 30 years, but this longer duration does not affect the novel's insistence on the spatialisation of narrative (and city) time: as 'the rapid succession of narrative lines also corresponds to movements in space, the whole urban structure is elliptically suggested' (96).

Also published in 1955, Donald Heiney's 'Illiers and Combray: a study in literary geography' is an early work on the literary side which challenges the idea that critical work in literary studies on geographical themes only began after the 1980s. Heiney's article is a work of Proustian criticism, reconsidering the connections linking the historical Illiers and the fictional Combray and arguing that it is 'precisely a study of the relation between [the] two realms – between "experiential sources" and "creative and imaginative sources" – which 'will lead us to an understanding of Proust's method'. According to Heiney, what he calls the 'literary geography' of the Illiers-Combray problem is 'at the very base of Proustian criticism' (17). Heiney's interest in the creative process establishes this article as an early work in the geographies of creativity and authorship which highlights the importance for literary criticism of investigating the distinctions between the tangible and the 'phantom' earlier noted by Virginia Woolf. 'Combray,' Heiney argues, 'had a reality quite apart from physical substance', and while the literary tourist might merge the two worlds in their own experience, the distinction between the two was crucial for Proust, who used the distinction between Illiers and Combray for 'aesthetic and technical' reasons, separating his childhood experience from the recollections of his adult life and strengthening the impression that his childhood had been 'merely an illusory dream' (25).

The work of Raymond Williams, particularly *The Country and the City* (1973), is often considered a seminal text for literary geography within literary studies, although the impact of *The Country and the City* on geographical work with literary texts seems mostly to have been made indirectly through cultural studies and cultural geography as a whole, and it goes generally unmentioned in geographical reviews of the field. In the US, Edward Marcotte's 'The space of the novel', which appeared in the *Partisan Review* in 1974, represents the early stages of a developing but sporadic interest within US-based literary studies in questions of space and literary setting, which would be further expanded with Leonard Lutwack's 1984 *The Role of Place in Literature*. D.C.D. Pocock mentions the work of both Marcotte and Lutwack in his 1988 review article on 'Geography and literature' for *Progress in Human Geography*.

THE AMERICAN LANDSCAPE IN AMERICAN STUDIES 1950–1979

The interdisciplinary field of American Studies, established mid-century in the USA, produced several early works linking American literature to geographical themes, well before what would become known as 'the spatial turn' in cultural and literary studies. The early 'myth and symbol' school of work in American Studies is notable for its exploration of connections between US national history, American exceptionalism, landscape, space and place, and many of those early works have had an impact on the development of contemporary literary geography. Henry Nash Smith's *Virgin Land: The American West as Symbol and Myth* (1950), often considered to have launched the field of American Studies, was originally a doctoral dissertation in Harvard's new (1937) History of American Civilization programme. Smith's work connects the literary expression of the myths and symbols of the Euro-American west with their impact on contemporary politics, economics, and society. Leo Marx's *The Machine in the Garden: Technology and the Pastoral Ideal in America*, a second key text for American Studies, was also originally a Harvard American Studies doctoral dissertation. It was first published as an article in 1956 and then in book form in 1964. John Conron's *The American Landscape: A Critical Anthology of Prose and Poetry* appeared in 1973, the first of Annette Kolodny's feminist readings of US literature and geography, *The Lay of the Land*, came out in 1975, and Alan Trachtenberg's *Brooklyn Bridge: Fact and Symbol*, based on his 1962 Minnesota doctoral dissertation, was published in 1979.

'GEOGRAPHY AND LITERATURE' POSTWAR TO 1970

In John Kerrigan's 1998 version of the history of human geography and its interest in literature, postwar geography was a '"spatial science", free from the approximation of language and the bias of subjectivity' (3). Nevertheless, H.C. Darby's 1948 article in *Geographical Review* on 'The regional geography of Thomas Hardy's Wessex' remains a particularly well-known and regularly cited example of a work in literary geography from the immediate postwar years. Darby's article is of historiographical interest in literary geography for two reasons: first, it counters the idea that postwar geography was practised solely as a positivist and quantitative spatial science, with no interest in the literary; and second, it forms part of a longstanding and still active interdisciplinary interest in Hardy's Wessex that can be traced at least as far back as 1902. Work on Hardy's Wessex thus provides some useful examples of how literary geography in the 20th century functioned as a coherent, collaborative (and sometimes combative) cross-referenced project. Clearly, not all of the map-related work in literary geography in this era was of the kind Kerrigan was referring to when he dismissed the 'amiable books [that] have been written about Hardy's Wessex and the Brontës' Haworth' (4).

Closely following H.C. Darby's 1948 work on the regional geography of Wessex, several more articles further complicate Kerrigan's assessment of postwar geography as a discipline hostile to considerations of language and subjectivity. Other articles in the area of literary geography from the 1960s continued the long tradition of work on the links that connected the novel with the geography of regions and regionalism, while Barry N. Floyd's 'Toward a more literary geography' (1961) published in *The Professional Geographer*, was primarily concerned with 'the role of good writing in the presentation of geography'. Like J.K. Wright before him, he emphasised the value of the subjective in geographical scholarship. His rebuttal of Richard Hartshorne's (1939) argument that literary description is incompatible with the objectivity required of geographers extends J.K. Wright's openness to the subjective, and prefigures many of the concerns, values, and practices that would subsequently emerge in postpositivist cultural geography.

THE 1970S

The growing presence of literary geography as a geographical subfield in the 1970s is indicated by two connected developments. First, expanding interest in working with literary texts started to become visible in conference programmes. The 1972 meeting of the International Geographical Union, for example, included a session on the use of the novel in teaching regional geography. Then in 1974 the annual meeting of the Association of American Geographers included a session on landscape in literature. In 1979 the Institute of British Geographers launched a series of sessions for its annual meetings 'on the intentionally broader perspective of geography and literature'. These sessions, which continued into the 1980s, are summarised in a series of reports for the journal *Area* on geography and literature at the conferences of the Institute of British Geographers. Second, literary geography articles routinely began to include review sections on the history of the subfield in general, and the first collections of essays on 'geography and literature' or 'landscape in literature' started to appear. In 1977, for example, Christopher L. Salter and William J. Lloyd's 'Landscape in literature' was published in the Association for American Geographers' series of Resource Papers for College Geography. In their introduction, Salter and Lloyd explain that they had written the resource paper 'in hopes of generating additional enthusiasm within geography for the wealth of landscape insights found in creative literature' (iv). The volume ends with an appendix listing 'selected reference works for landscape in literature'.

'LANDSCAPE IN LITERATURE' BECOMES 'LITERARY GEOGRAPHY'

Although Salter and Lloyd's 1977 resource paper dealt with 'landscape in literature', the field had already acquired what would become its contemporary name – literary geography – a year earlier, in 1976, in the title of the MA thesis of one of the pioneers of literary geography, Ramesh Dhussa: 'The perception of home and external regions through the writings of Sarat Chandra Chatterjee: a study in literary geography'. In the same year, Dhussa and co-author A.K. Dutt published 'The contrasting image and landscape of Calcutta through literature' in the *Proceedings of the Association of American Geographers*. Dhussa's naming of the field was consolidated in his 1979 article for *The Deccan Geographer*, 'Commentary on "literary geography"' and then in 1981 he published the early review article, 'Literary geography: a bibliography' in the *Journal of Cultural Geography*. Dhussa's research interests tended to focus on images of Indian cities: his 'Literary geography and changing aspects of Calcutta', again co-authored with Dutt, came out in 1981 in *New Perspectives in Geography*. This interest was further pursued in his 2012 book chapter 'Geographic images of Old Delhi through literature' and two more co-authored works on Sarat Chandra, both subtitled 'A literary geographic study', which came out in 1981 (*Geojournal*) and 1983 (*The National Geographical Journal of India*). Dhussa's second review article, this time co-authored with Allen G. Noble, 'Image and substance: A review of literary geography', was published in the *Journal of Cultural Geography* in 1990.

Two chapters in the 1976 collection *Environmental Knowing: Theories, Research and Methods* (Moore and Golledge, eds) show that literary geography was beginning to be included in agenda-setting discussions of geographical theory and practice more broadly. Contributions to the collection covered both methodology and current research topics, with the unifying theme being the way in which the human mind organises the spatial world. The various chapters concentrated on two overlapping problems: orientation in space; and the assignment of meaning to place. The two literary chapters were David Seamon's on the 'Phenomenological investigation of imaginative literature: a commentary' and 'Literature, experience and environmental knowing', contributed by Yi-Fu Tuan, another cultural geographer who has had a strong impact on the development of literary geography.

Other significant work in literary geography which appeared in the 1970s included Christopher Salter's chapter 'Signatures and settings: one approach to landscape in literature', included in Karl Butzer's edited collection *Dimensions of Human Geography* in 1978, as well as early articles in Charles Aiken's run of studies of Faulkner's fictional Yoknapatawpha Country in the *Geographical Review*, a series which culminated in his 2009 monograph *William Faulkner and the Southern Landscape*. D.C.D. Pocock's influential body of work on literary geography also began to appear in the 1970s, starting with his article on 'The novelist's image of the North' published in *Transactions of the Institute of British Geographers* in 1979. This article prompted a responding comment article in the same journal in 1980, in which Alec Paul and Paul Simpson-Housley expanded the discussion while agreeing that 'regional definition, one of the traditional cornerstones of geography, remains a vital task', with literature, film and television functioning as major contributors to regional image (386). Work in literary geography on children's literature, mysteries and popular fiction was also beginning to become established in geography journals in this era, and there was early evidence of work on literary geography in Australia, with D.N. Jeans' 'Some literary examples of humanistic descriptions of place' appearing in *The Australian Geographer* in 1979.

HUMANISTIC LITERARY GEOGRAPHY

In his introduction to the essays collected in *Humanistic Geography and Literature* (1981), D.C.D. Pocock goes some way to anticipating Kerrigan's later explanation that humanistic geography turned toward literature in the 1970s in reaction to the positivist and quantitative geographies that were mainstream at the time, but he differs from it on one key point: where Kerrigan portrays geographical work with literary texts in the 1970s as a something new, an experiment (which ultimately failed), Pocock presents it as simply the latest resurgence of a subfield tradition that had been sustained since at least the 1920s. 'Disillusioned by an era of logical positivism, maybe shell-shocked by the quantitative revolution, perhaps rediscovering the literary heritage of geography' (9), whatever the reason, literary geography was entering a new phase, and humanistic work with literary texts was not so much a new turn toward the literary within geography but rather an extension of the line of work on subjectivity, the imagination, and literary texts first established by J.K. Wright in the 1920s.

THE 1980S

In addition to Pocock's edited collection, the 1980s included two particularly significant articles on Hardy's literary geographies, both in prominent geography journals: geographer Brian Birch's 'Wessex, Hardy, and the nature novelists' (1981) and literary scholar John Barrell's 'Geographies of Hardy's Wessex' (1982). It is also worth pointing out that despite Kerrigan's claim that geographers avoided works dealing with the 'disorientations of modernity' several articles on literary geography and modernist fiction were published in the 1970s and 80s. J.D. Porteous, for example, published two articles on Malcolm Lowry: 'Inscape: landscapes of the mind in the Canadian and Mexican novels of Malcolm Lowry' (1986) and 'Deathscape: Malcolm Lowry's topophobic view of the city' (1987), both in the *Canadian Geographer/Le Géographe canadien*. Brian Robinson's work on literary texts also emphasised the importance of spatial fragmentation, arguing that 'as a perspective on the world, although it may not have been admitted into the canon of a positivist-scientific approach, [it] has been a common aspect of twentieth century literature and art' (1977: 549).

In addition to single articles and book chapters, more reviews and collections continued to appear in 1980s. Published in 1987, the interdisciplinary collection of essays edited by William E. Mallory and Paul Simpson-Housley, *Geography and Literature*, included work by creative writers, literary critics and geographers. While a central concern in the collection was the importance of literature to ideas of region, in the final essay, 'The geography of a crossroads: modernism, surrealism and geography', Brian Robinson (again) asks several prescient questions about literary geography, including the extent to which 'movements' have a geography and the possibility of 'a geography that would not merely use literature as a source' (Mallory and Simpson-Housley, 1987: xv).

The following year, 1988, saw the publication of a review article in the prominent journal *Progress in Human Geography* by D.C.D. Pocock on 'Geography and literature', suggesting that by the late 1980s literary geography had become established as part of the mainstream. The same year saw the publication of a special 'focus' section in *the Canadian Geographer/Le Géographe canadien* on 'Literary landscapes: geography and literature' which included an introduction and four short articles. 'The study of geography and literature is undergoing a revival while at a crossroads', the editors explain,

> the search for literary imagery of a factual and fictional basis to illustrate the characteristics of landscapes and regions ... is being complemented by analyses of literary landscapes as metaphors and symbols ... as tourism resources ... as teaching tools ... as social history ... and as a medium of popular culture.
>
> (Sandberg and Marsh, 1988: 266)

Shortly thereafter, the *Journal of Cultural Geography* published the 1990 review by Noble and Dhussa: 'Image and substance: a review of literary geography', and then in 1994 *Progress in Human Geography* published Marc Brosseau's 'Geography's literature'.

LITERARY GEOGRAPHY IN THE 20TH CENTURY: MORE THAN A 'WRONG TURN'

In the 1998 essay in which he argued for a 'new' literary geography John Kerrigan spent most of his column inches reviewing five books, none of them by geographers working on literary texts. Two of the books reviewed were Brian Jarvis's *Postmodern Cartographies* and Franco Moretti's *Atlas of the European Novel 1800–1900*, both published in 1998 by scholars working in literary studies; the remaining three books were published in 1997 in the Arnold series of readers in geography: *Space, Gender, Knowledge, Undoing Place?* and *Reading Human Geography*. Kerrigan points out that with 'space' becoming an increasingly important concept in literary and cultural studies 'there is obviously much to be said for consulting the geographers, who have made it their specialism' (4). Meanwhile he took Jarvis and Moretti's works as evidence of 'how a new synthesis might be made' involving literary criticism and geography, despite pointing out that Moretti

> ignores the kind of geography which literary critics can most easily learn from: the work done by Doreen Massey and others on how places are made through often fractious multi-scale processes which are not contained by particular locations and which involve a host of written and spoken practices.
>
> (Kerrigan, 1998: 4)

Massey's work has indeed had a significant influence on literary geography, but the way in which Kerrigan's essay looks towards geography in general and not contemporary literary geography is typical of work in literary studies as it began to embrace questions of space and place in the 1990s.

While his suggestion that literary critics should consult geographers as they develop a new literary geography was in some senses positive, Kerrigan's outline of the history of literary geography unfortunately extended the gap between geographical work on literary texts and work on geographical themes in literary studies, taking a single collection from the early 1980s as a sample text, not mentioning the important work that had been (and was being) published in geographical journals, and characterising the field as something that sprang to life in the 1970s and then fizzled out. Given that literary geography, under one name or another, had been in development within human geography since the late 19th century, his concluding reference to 'the emerging subject of literary geography' reveals the gap in mutual understanding which separated literary critics and geographers as the 20th century drew to a close.

2

AIMS AND METHODS

The key point about the aims and methods of contemporary literary geography is that they are multiple and various, held in workable tension by a shared commitment to the basic principles of literary geography as it has developed from its human geography origins in collaboration with work in literary studies. In fact, the variety of aims and methods in contemporary literary geography is the inevitable result of its roots in two very different academic traditions and a testament to its lively interdisciplinarity. The deep historical extent of literary geography as a geographical subfield, together with its contemporary breadth across a wide range of related disciplines, means that a tightly circumscribed and integrated core set of purposes and approaches would not only be very difficult to achieve but also counterproductive. Literary geographers are only now beginning to explore in detail both their historiographical roots and the potential of more active collaboration involving not only geographers and literary critics but also participants from associated fields such as the digital humanities, cartography, place writing and geopoetics.

Envisioning literary geography as a networked collective as opposed to a sharply defined field with a fixed set of shared aims and methods is not the same thing as saying that the kind of

DOI: 10.4324/9781315778273-3

literary geography discussed here includes all academic work involving literary text and geographical/spatial themes, or indeed all work which describes itself as literary geography. As explained in the introduction, the literary geography outlined in this book is identified not by a specific label (which has been applied at various times to various other kinds of writing, both popular and academic) but by reference to a distinct tradition, which has at its core an interest not only in the human environment and literary texts as interconnected objects of research, but also in the aims and methods of human geography and literary studies.

WRITING THE INTERDISCIPLINE

Even before the intensification of interest in active collaboration involving literary critics and human geographers which began to re-energise literary geography in the late 20th century, there was a history of scholars located in one of the disciplines publishing in venues associated with the other: in literary studies, John Barrell, for example, engaged with the 'other' disciplinary audience when he published his 'Geographies of Hardy's Wessex' in the *Journal of Historical Geography* in 1982. Barrell's earlier monograph *The Idea of Landscape and the Sense of Place 1730–1840: An Approach to the Poetry of John Clare*, while positioned within literary studies, is also a significant work for literary geography. Similarly, when the human geographer Mike Crang turned his interest in qualitative methods and cultural tourism toward literary geography, he published some of that work in literary studies venues. His article 'Placing stories, performing places: spatiality in Joyce and Austen', for example, was published in the 2008 volume of *Anglia: Zeitschrift für Englische Philologie*, a quarterly journal which publishes work on English linguistics, literature in English, and comparative literature. The same issue included an article by Marc Brosseau on Charles Bukowski's short stories. It is also an important point that not all work in literary geography is contributed by people working within a single discipline: several scholars in the field locate their research at and across disciplinary boundaries and emphasise a fluid disciplinarity. Some authors have been able to evade any need to identify with a 'primary' disciplinary position by working in programmes or departments which are themselves interdisciplinary.

Work in literary geography today typically performs its commitment to the interdiscipline's core interests by pursuing a triple aim: to add to geographical knowledge and theory; to contribute critical insights into literary genres, movements, authors and works; and to participate in the consolidation of literary geography as a collective project by referring to and building on its distinctive historiography. James Kneale articulates this set of aims in the introduction to his chapter in *The Transgressive Iain Banks* (2013), opening his discussion of the literary geography of Iain Banks with two 'confessions' – the first, 'I have never been to the gas giant Nasqueron', is a nod to John Barrell's 'Geographies of Hardy's Wessex' (1982), which begins with the admission: 'I have never been to Dorset.' By citing Barrell's work, Kneale not only makes the point that both Nasqueron and Wessex are invented and fictional, but also deliberately locates his writing within the literary geography tradition. Kneale's second 'confession' has to do with his position as a geographer writing for a collection dominated by authors working in literary studies:

> The second [confession] is that I am a geographer, which inevitably affects the way I approach literature.... . On the one hand I want to suggest that thinking about space can develop new critical insights into Iain Banks' fiction; on the other hand, thinking about literature can also help us theorize the representation and experience of space.
> (2013: 45)

While current work in literary geography often shares the three aims articulated explicitly and implicitly here by Kneale, there naturally have been and still are many cases in which scholars working within the broad range of literary geography have prioritised more specific disciplinary aims. For geographers, the specific aims and methods of work with literary texts have shifted considerably over the past hundred years, in line with larger developments in geography as a whole. Appreciation of the extent of this depth and variation is easily lost in contemporary understandings of literary geography, however, not least because as an interdiscipline it has so far produced few thoroughly detailed historiographical reviews. New initiatives, responding to emerging themes, practices and goals in geography and literary studies, are of course always exciting; but at the same time more work on the back-story of literary geography would add nuance to narratives which have oversimplified its history and repressed its complexity. Without a shared awareness of the density and detail of the history and range of literary geography it is too easy for new work to assume that a particular aim or method is central or obvious, and to critique other work for not achieving that aim or following that method, without considering what exactly that other work set out to do, and how its aims and methods connect to the depth and breadth of the field as a whole.

VARIETY IN AIMS AND METHODS

Aims and methods in literary geography, then, have varied enormously over time and according to the way work has emerged out of its contributing disciplines. In the very early days of geography's development as a discipline, for example, literary texts were frequently promoted as important because of their ability to stimulate geographical visualisation. In a 1902 article for *Geography*, M.W. Keatinge stressed the value of bringing poetry into the geography classroom, arguing that an urgent task for the geography teacher was 'the quickening of the geographical imagination' and including several examples of poems able to provide 'a general tone and background of scenic emotion', something he termed an essential part of geography teaching and not to be 'cavilled at as extraneous matter' (1902: 147, 149).

Keatinge's 1902 article thus also shows a very early example of the way in which geographical interest in literary texts has been linked to classroom teaching. The aim of geographical engagement with literary texts has varied greatly since then, as aims and methods in geography in general have gone through major changes in the past century. Working with literary texts has always been just one of a wide range of possible methods available for human geographers, which means that it is important to recognise that geographers working with literary texts are not likely to be primarily concerned with making a contribution to literary criticism. So where Andrew Thacker's 'critical literary geography' (2005) was designed to be a fresh approach in literary criticism, Joanne Sharp's 'Towards a critical analysis of fictive geographies' (2000) argued for a literary geography able to work with 'uninformed' public readings as well as with the skilled close readings of the literary critic – insisting that without this dimension the literary geographer focused purely on close reading 'must assume either that all read the complexities of the text with the same informed skills, or that the academic interpretation is somehow more valid than other possible readings' (332). That 'valid' works in the context of academic geography because the production of 'sophisticated' readings is not a uniformly prime concern for literary geographers. Where 'critical' for Thacker refers to the close critical readings performed within academic literary criticism, for Sharp 'critical' refers to the need to think critically about literary texts from a geographical perspective. As these very different understandings of 'critical literary geography' suggest, while interdisciplinary collaborations in general tend to have a complex range of aims and methods, some of them congenial and others at odds, that range becomes even further stretched in a social science/humanities combination.

A brief look at four themes in literary geography should be able to provide some sense of the historical depth and current breadth of aims and methods in literary geography. The first theme is the very traditional theme of 'the idea of the region'. The three which follow are 'conventions and innovations in geographic writing styles', 'creative writing in the geography classroom' and 'geographies of gender'. All four of these themes also indicate the way in which literary geography tends to be produced at the overlap of the humanities and the social sciences, and at the meeting point of creativity, imagination, analysis and the lived environment.

THE IDEA OF THE REGION

Because of the importance of regional geography to the early development of human geography, the regional novel was a key literary genre in the early years of literary geography. Initially, geographers tended to work with 19th-century realist fiction, not necessarily because of any preference for that mode of writing, but because the realist regional novel was both a representation of regional consciousness and at the same time an important factor in its development. This led to later critical commentaries from both geographers and literary critics assuming that this interest in realist fiction came from a naïve understanding of the regional novel as the fictional equivalent of fieldwork. In his various explorations of the importance of literature for the human geographer Yi-Fu Tuan complicates this reductive view of the reasons why literary geographers gravitated towards realist fiction with his 1978 explanation of three of the ways in which literature 'serves the geographer': first, as a thought experiment, directing geographical attention to various modes of human existence; second, as an artefact providing access to the environmental perceptions and values of particular cultures; third, as an 'ambitious attempt to balance the subjective and the objective' which could function as 'a model for geographical synthesis' (1978: 205). It is in relation to this last point that Tuan explains the appeal of the 19th-century realist novel for geographers; the point is not that they were looking for fictionalised field notes, but rather that 'the Victorian novel and its 20th century progenies show how it is possible to combine in one work individuals and social types, the inchoate density of living and explicit analyses, points of view, and an objective reality', thus providing a model for geographical writing (205).

CONVENTIONS AND INNOVATIONS IN GEOGRAPHIC WRITING STYLES

Tuan's reference here to the attraction of the 19th-century regional novel emphasises one of the most enduring connections between aims and methods in human geography and its interest in literary texts: the interplay between literary and geographical writing styles. This has been a feature of literary geography since its earliest days, and has most recently resurfaced in cultural geography's 'creative (re)turn', a theme taken up in more detail in

Chapter 5. Debate over the appropriateness of various writing styles in geography, on 'creative writing' as a method, and on 'completeness' and 'synthesis' as aims for geographers, is still active and currently ranging across a wide range of topics from place writing to deep mapping. For example, while Tuan emphasised the way in which 19th-century realist fiction was able to provide 'a model for geographical synthesis', Ewart Johns, in an article published in *Geography* nearly two decades earlier, had called the idea that 'synthesis is the aim of creative writing in geography' a serious mistake (1960: 176). Johns proposed that geographical studies in the postwar era, which still held 'regional studies as an ultimate goal', had arrived at 'a point where the reconsideration of its basic technique is essential'. He argued that creative geographical writing is an art, and thus quite different to synthesis, his point being that geographical writing in its more creative modes, 'does not aim at completeness, or even have completeness as one of its essential components' (176).

CREATIVE WRITING IN THE GEOGRAPHY CLASSROOM

The impulse to integrate creative writing into geographical aims and methods has always been linked to the classroom, originally in the reading of descriptive texts and more recently also by encouraging creative writing. J.K. Wright (1924), for example, like M.W. Keatinge before him, trusted the 'highly developed geographical sense' of some authors and their ability to visualise and describe regional geographies, and emphasised the way in which literary description helped to 'make the world really alive to students of geography' (1924: 659). The value of creative writing in its ability to engage students of all ages in the geography classroom has been a particularly persistent theme in literary geography: the 1972 meeting of the International Geographical Union, for example, included a session on novels and geography teaching, and more recently the journal *Geography*, aimed at lecturers, teachers and students in post-16 geography, included a themed section on geography and poetry (2008). The essays in this section encouraged creative writing in the classroom: geographer Hayden Lorimer, for example, urged geographers to pay more attention to various creative writing activities, including poetry. In her introduction to the section, Eleanor Rawling suggests that 'such activities could have immense educational potential, reminding us that writing about, for, and in place should surely not just be left to poets but should be at the heart of being a geographer. Geography as creative writing?' (2008: 171)

In 2011 the critical geography journal ACME published 'The bus hub', a song/poem submitted by geographer Kafui Attoh in both print and audio formats. In its final published form 'The bus hub' was accompanied by an editorial introduction and two commentaries. The editor's introduction (Butz, 2011: 278–279) included an edited version of Attoh's reaction to those observations, which usefully highlight some of the issues surrounding the question of activist writing and academic analysis in critical literary geography, a classification which in this case denotes literary geography as a method in critical geography:

> After reading both commentaries, what is striking is how differently I see my own work ... In the classroom setting, the poem and song have been far better at eliciting comments on issues of public transit and urban space in Syracuse than anything I have written academically ... [In this context] I find it striking to then read commentaries, which return the debate to ... academic language ... Ultimately, in encouraging free commentary I have also encouraged commentary that I do not necessarily understand nor, in moments, agree with ... [Nevertheless] I think they reflect what I see as the value of the poem, which has, from my classroom experience, always been about sparking debate and discussion, even if I do not necessarily agree with all that is being said.
>
> (279)

GEOGRAPHIES OF GENDER

Modes of geographical writing connect with another ongoing theme in human geography: the link between discourse and gender in geographical knowledge production, and the historic tendency to discount ways of knowing and writing styles which deviate from a normative white masculine and middle-class position. Although there has been some confusion in literary studies over the era in which gender emerged as a concern in human geography, it is not in fact a recent theme and has been of rising importance in the mainstream since the 1970s. The source of the confusion seems to be a remark made in 1994 by Doreen Massey that when she was a student 'these things were just not talked about' (187). Best known in literary geography today for her spatial theory, particularly 'A global sense of place' (1991) and *For Space* (2005), Massey was here referring to the absence of interest in gender and geography in the era in which she started her studies, which would have been some time in the 1960s, well before the publication of her *Space, Place and Gender* in 1994.

Ten years before that, in 1984, the Royal Geographical Society/Institute of British Geographers Women and Geography Study Group (founded in 1980; it is now the Gender and Feminist Geographies Research Group) had published *Gender and Geography*; Gillian Rose's *Feminism and Geography* came out in 1993. *Gender, Place and Culture: A Journal of Feminist Geography*, which has been engaging with 'gender issues in human geography' since 1994, has included some significant work on literary geography and gender, including Clive Barnett's '"A choice of nightmares": narration and desire in *Heart of Darkness*', which deals with its 'gendered organisation of narration' and argues that Conrad's text 'fictionalises its audience as an exclusively masculine community of readers, bounded together by shared interests and commitments' (277). Garth Myers' 'Colonial Geography and Masculinity in Eric Dutton's *Kenya Mountain*' (2002) performs a reading of the book grounded in 'recent feminist and progressive analyses of gender, colonial geography and adventure writing', while Joanna Surgeoner's 'A feminist literary cartography of the Canadian north: women, writing and place in Aritha van Herk's *Places Far From Ellesmere*' (2007) argues that 'van Herk's insistence upon the power of feminist textual rereadings, an insistence that results from her aversion to authority, critically shapes her geographical imaginary, and her understanding of North' (641).

DEVELOPING A MUTUAL REGARD

Given what Ewart Johns might appreciate as a permanent state of dynamic incompleteness, the kind of broad-ranging literary geography practised today could perhaps be viewed as something of an academic art: a collective practice characterised by an organic openness that cannot easily be contained by taxonomies, lists, and systematic organisation. While the journal *Literary Geographies* offers the interdiscipline an integrated venue for sharing and communicating this expansive and expanding body of work, publication of mixed literary/geographical work in single-discipline journals nevertheless remains productive, not only by situating literary geography in high-profile disciplinary journals but also by appealing to scholars not familiar with the field of literary geography who would have no reason to go straight to the interdisciplinary venue. Crossover publication, in which (for example) a geographer publishes in a literary studies journal, has been and continues to be vital for the development of the active interdiscipline. Outreach of all kinds from literary geographers will remain important to the maintenance and development of the field, which has in the past been severely impeded by splits in motivation, practice and mutual understanding, dividing work on literature and geo-spatial themes in human geography from related work in literary criticism, particularly during the early stages of the 'spatial turn' in literary studies. As one of the major difficulties at this time was the unfamiliarity of literary studies with the existing (geographical) form of literary geography, its historiography, aims and practice, there is good reason for geographers to continue publishing in more literary venues.

Before the 1990s and early 2000s, at a time when very few literary critics published work in geography journals, they nonetheless contributed from a distance to the four-way interdisciplinary intersection at the heart of literary geography, because of the work they published as literary studies. Although not entirely unknown, direct participation of literary critics in any collaborative literary-geographical project was understandably rare in this era, given that until the 1980s there was little extended interest within literary studies in the interdisciplinary combination which powered the literary geography of human geographers – not only literary texts and natural or built environments, but also work in both literary studies and human geography. Actual research collaborations bringing literary critics (and not just their published work) into the kind of literary geography which included a strong geographical component only started to become conceivable in the 1990s and early 2000s, as literary and cultural studies began their turn toward geographical themes and spatialities. As explained in the previous chapter, the first moves towards practical collaboration were held back at this stage by knowledge gaps and misunderstandings.

It is important to point out that the aims and methods of literary geography have not necessarily always been well understood or respected within geography as a whole, which means that geographers themselves bear some responsibility for the gaps and misunderstandings which discouraged literary critics from engaging earlier with geographical work on literary texts. In the course of the 20th century, as the mainstream human geography tradition moved from environmental determinism, through attempts to establish human geography as a spatial science, and then on into positivism and the quantitative revolution, geographical work with literary texts was never central. With the emergence of humanistic geography and its emphasis on the subjective perception of place and space in the 1970s literary geography began to gain some mainstream traction, and then further opportunities for recognition came with the rise of what was known at the time as the 'new' cultural geography in the 1980s; both initiatives in cultural geography, however, were themselves the subject of intra-disciplinary debate, and doubts about the effectiveness of geographical work with literature remained. Perhaps due to some form of disciplinary deference, remarks made by geographers about the literary geography subfield have at times suggested that geographers engaging with literary text were something of a disciplinary embarrassment and that their work would naturally lack sophistication in comparison with that of literary critics. So it is worth noting that while John Kerrigan and Andrew Thacker appeared to have little interest in the history of geography's literary geography, they may well have been directly or indirectly influenced in this direction, paradoxically, by geographers.

INTRADISCIPLINARY DIFFICULTIES

In a surprisingly recent example of this lack of regard for literary geography *within* geography, the geographer reviewing Thomas O. Beebee's *Nation and Region in Modern American and European Fiction* for *Comparative Literary Studies* in 2011 remarked that 'there is in my discipline a subfield called the geography of literature. But it is not very good.' The review dismisses work on the geography of literature as tending 'to turn on such mundane activities as plotting Thomas Hardy's fictional Wessex on to nonfictional West England county maps' (Barnes, 2011: 254) Actually, by 2011, even in the limited area of work dealing with Hardy's Wessex, there were several examples of work in literary geography that went well beyond the plotting of fictional setting on to nonfictional maps, at least three of them published in mainstream geography journals: the *Geographical Review* (1948), *Transactions of the Institute of British Geography* (1981) and the *Journal of Historical Geography* (1982).

Even H.C. Darby's 1948 'The regional geography of Thomas Hardy's Wessex', a very early geographical work on Hardy, was not limited to mundane plotting; as with much early literary geography, its focus was on the theme of the region in human geography:

> One of the main features in the development of modern geographical thought has been the increasing importance attached to the idea of the region. But the regional approach has not been the monopoly of academic geographers. On the contrary it seems to have been an element of the mental climate since the middle of the nineteenth century, which has manifested itself in a variety of ways – political, economic, cultural. One expression has been the rise of the regional novel as a literary form.
>
> (426)

In 1981, geographer Brian Birch took a slightly different regional studies approach which allowed him to widen the focus from Hardy to other Wessex writers, arguing that although in general work on Hardy's geographies had concentrated on his 'use of settings from the real region to create his part-imaginary Wessex', there were other aspects to his 'topographic approach' that were of equal interest, such as 'his attempts in his later novels to move his stories across different districts within Wessex', a socio-ecological approach also taken by lesser known writers, thereby enabling them to attract a readership based on the idea of the fictional Wessex as a 'known region' (348). Then John Barrell opened his 1982 article by declaring he had never been to Dorset:

> not to disqualify myself from writing this essay, but to indicate at the outset the sort of essay it will not be. It will not be concerned with the identification of places in the Wessex novels with their possible originals in Dorset and the neighbouring counties.
>
> (347)

Instead, Barrell argued that the novels of Thomas Hardy 'represent a number of different "geographies" – the means by which their various characters and narrators explore places and come to know them'. Barrell distinguishes the geographies of characters from those of the narrators, explaining (for example) that the geography of Tess and other inhabitants of Egdon Heath (*Tess of the d'Urbevilles*), 'is represented as circular, and is constructed by more senses than the visual, while that of the reader is linear and wholly visual in its preoccupations with geology, cartography and the picturesque' (347). Barrell also points out that the idea of the 'local', while available to the reader, is an impossible concept for characters for whom the local constitutes the whole, thus introducing the concept of internal/external geographies or character vs narrator/reader spatial understanding.

The articles on Hardy's Wessex published by Darby, Birch and Barrell between 1948 and 1982 testify to a far greater complexity in the geographical approach to literary texts than that suggested by the 2011 review in *Comparative Literature*. And although the reviewer concludes his discussion of Beebee's *Nation and Region in Modern American and European Fiction* by suggesting that geographers could learn a great deal from efforts being made in comparative literature to provide a theoretical framework for work on geographical themes and literary texts, Barrell's 1982 article made a strong theoretical contribution to literary geography, offering an early version of the idea that fiction could be understood as something which happens in temporo-spatial interactions. The view of literature as a collaboration involving author, reader, characters and other active agents, spread across space and time, and involving both the fictional world and the world of production and reception, is implicit in Barrell's argument. This focus on processes of collaboration would later (but still before the *Comparative Literature* review) become an important theoretical framework for literary geography first through the idea of the 'text as a spatial event' and later in relational literary geography. The reviewer, however, arguing that Beebee's wide-ranging work 'makes those geographical Wessex studies appear parochial and narrow' (Barnes, 2011: 254) emphasised the 'potential for an interesting collusion of comparative literature with geography' and ends with a call to 'let the conversation begin'. This is much the same line as that taken earlier by John Kerrigan, who dismissed the human geography tradition of literary geography as a failed experiment, instead promoting the value of spatial theory more generally. This criticism misses at least three important points: first, that literary geographers have always positioned their work in relation to the flow of broader debate within geography; second, that by the time the 2011 review was written literary geographers had been using geographical theory for some time to develop a theoretical framework for their work; and third, that literary geographers were already attempting to integrate their work into literary studies, or at least to make their work known outside human geography, by publishing in literary journals and edited collections.

CROSS-DISCIPLINARY DIFFICULTIES

By 2011, then, literary geographers were already concerned with building new frameworks for the field by drawing on a broad range of work not only in human geography and spatial theory but also in literary theory and work on reading practices. Marc Brosseau's 1994 review article 'Geography's literature' is a case in point, as is his entry on the history and theoretical framing of literary geography for the 2009 *International Dictionary of Human Geography*. Joanne Sharp's 'Towards a critical analysis of fictive geographies', for *Area*, made a fundamental contribution to the theoretical framing of literary geography; the 2008 *Geography Compass* review essay 'Text as it happens' used Doreen Massey's work on space and place to suggest a spatially-theorised way of dealing with different approaches to literary geography; and Angharad Saunders' review article for the journal *Progress in Human Geography*, 'Literary geography: Reforging the connections' (2010), further negotiated important theoretical issues. Despite these relatively high-profile publications, a continued uncertain level of enthusiasm within human geography for its own subfield, added to unfamiliarity with its theoretical progress, is likely to have had a damaging impact on the way in which scholars in other fields have assessed its depth and potential. A tendency to belittle geographical work with literary texts and to defer to literary critics may go some way to explaining the absence of any engagement with the existing form of (geographical) literary geography in Andrew Thacker's 2005 article 'The idea of a critical literary geography', despite the fact that it was presented in pre-published form at the annual conference of the Royal Geographical Society in 2004, in the session 'Textual Spaces, Spatial Texts'.

In their editorial introduction to the 2005 volume of *New Formations* which included several papers from that RGS conference session, including Thacker's, geographer Richard Phillips and his literary studies colleague Scott McCracken note that

> Cross-disciplinary misunderstandings are the inevitable consequences of differences in perspective, language and values: of different critical literacies. As editors we have had vigorous debates about the issue, debates coloured by our different disciplinary perspectives which changed in character and emphasis according to the spaces in which

they were situated at the time. The conference, for example, took place on geographical terrain, while the editorial process was conducted in the context of a journal which includes culture, theory and politics, but not geography, in its title.

(8)

The kinds of misunderstandings and differences Phillips and McCracken note remain a major challenge for the development of literary geography. As the interdiscipline experiences an increase in interest and activity, basic questions about *what literary geography is* and *what it can do* will become increasingly important if its various practitioners are going to be able to communicate. Even when discussion of these central questions took place only within human geography there were heated debates, in part because of the ways in which different positions related to broader disciplinary disputes about aims and methods. Now that spatial and geographical themes have been taken up across a broader range of disciplines it has become even more difficult to define the field in any straightforward way. In other words, the challenge now facing any attempt to create a consensus definition of the field comes not only from its complex historiography and its identity as a subfield in human geography but also from the urgent need to negotiate deep-seated diversity in purpose and practice across an interdisciplinary spectrum.

THE SPATIALITY OF LITERARY GEOGRAPHY

A basic openness to, and awareness of, the disparities in aims and methods within literary geography will continue to be necessary for the field as a whole if it is going to be able to generate and sustain some sense of connection and collective purpose. With literary geographies, plural, being practiced across an increasingly broad disciplinary range, reciprocal understanding of historiographies, objectives, terminologies and disciplinary practices will be vital to fostering the central ground of literary geography, singular, while helping to keep the more disciplinary ends of the larger continuum connected and in communication. How best to do this? There seem to be two main routes: to negotiate, somehow, an agreed central definition of theory, practice and terminology, and then police its borders; or to find an alternative method which relies on openness and mutual regard. To borrow the terms Doreen Massey uses to envision a 'global', rather than a bordered and parochial, 'sense of place', the choice seems to be between insisting on a unitary and contained centre or, alternatively, viewing the interdiscipline as something which happens, somewhat unpredictably, at the intersection of different paths.

The second view – of the interdiscipline as a dynamic 'meeting-up' of academic energies, permanently in process – was the one suggested by the review essay 'Text as it happens', which appeared in *Geography Compass* in 2008. Since publication, the article has primarily been cited as an articulation of the idea that texts come into being in the interactions of multiple agents (writers, editors, readers, critics and others). Nevertheless, its original primary purpose was to use this view of the spatiality of literary text as the theoretical basis for a broad and inclusive understanding of interdisciplinary literary geography. This framework was built on the article's argument that literary texts can be understood to come into being ('happen') in the interactions of participants typically separated in space and in time, an argument which depends on 'an explicitly spatial view of the writing–reading nexus as a contextualized and always emerging geographical event', the event being 'geographical' not primarily because it relates to physical locations, literal distances, or topography, but because it is a spatio-temporal process (Hones, 2008: 1301).

The key point for the framing of a collaborative literary geography which emerges from this view of the literary text is that it not only allows for multiple readings or approaches to specific literary texts, but that it also tolerates variation in textual interactions (readings, analyses, discussions) generated by different academic contexts. This makes conscious and informed attention to three points a prerequisite for understanding and evaluating the different ways of doing literary geography: (1) nuances of disciplinary context, (2) use of language and historiography, and (3) purpose and method.

Relying in this way on Doreen Massey's understanding of place, the article proposes the envisioning of literary geography as an interdiscipline in which the binding agent is not a sharply defined centre of established purposes and methods, but a shared awareness of and respect for the full range of current and emerging aims and methods. This enables it to provide

> a way of understanding and dealing with incompatible literary interpretations and also with irreconcilable approaches to literary geography. This openness to multiplicity develops from the point that text events are not only relational by nature and generated within social contexts in the initial encounter of author, text, and reader, but also only become publicly accessible when subsequently articulated within the mediating context of a particular social situation. The article proposes that literary geography as a collective endeavor can be developed and consolidated through an appreciation of the varying [disciplinary] contexts within which geographically oriented work with fiction is performed and articulated.
>
> (Hones, 2008: 1301)

Because 'Text as it happens' was written at a time when substantive collaboration involving literary critics and human geographers was only barely underway, the review portion of the article treated literary geography primarily as a long-standing subfield of human geography, while its forward-looking proposals were of necessity largely speculative. Nevertheless, its suggestions remain relevant:

> Literary geography has the potential to develop as a collective field energized by a sense of shared progress if scholars whose work engages with the geographies of text are willing to recognize the ways in which their own work is conditioned by context, to accept the validity of other contextually conditioned approaches, and to write as well as read across borders. Also critical will be the willingness of scholars working in related fields to cite, present, and publish adventurously, thereby locating their own work in multiple contexts, promoting cross-border thinking, and enabling the development of unprecedented but productive alliances and interactions. This will of

necessity have to be a somewhat circular process: the collective audience for literary geography as a whole will have to be generated in the process of being addressed.

(Hones, 2008: 1311)

The view of literary text as something which comes into being through spatial interaction is an approach to solving the challenge of literary geography's strong interdisciplinarity by providing a metadisciplinary framework within which spatial theory could enable various kinds of academic difference to be negotiated: in other words thinking spatially can enable not only new ways of reading texts but new ways of theorising the practice of interdisciplinary collaboration.

It is inevitably something of a trial to accept that no matter how clearly and unambiguously literary geographers attempt to express their research and thinking it will never be within their power to fully determine the ways in which that work is interpreted and used, especially beyond the disciplinary context of original production. While their ways of reading can to a degree be disciplined, their writings are out of their control once disseminated into the wider academy, where they will be read and used in unexpected ways. However, 'by taking responsibility for the production of meaning as readers', while 'abandoning the illusion of control as writers', literary geographers 'working together across the spectrum of the field could collaboratively generate a productive sense of community'. The process of identifying more clearly the various but overlapping spatial contexts and communities within which readings are not only generated and shared but also evaluated 'should make it easier for both analytic strategies and specific readings to be appreciated as the located products of particular collaborations and performative situations' (Hones, 2008: 1314).

CONCLUSION

The formation of a collaborative research core for literary geography will need sustained and careful work in developing awareness of and respect for the complex range of historiographies, aims, methods and terminologies which would have to coexist in a fully integrated interdiscipline. Continuing the argument underlying the historiographical reviews of the two previous chapters, this chapter on aims and methods has suggested that the best way to foster understanding and collaboration within the interdiscipline is to make literary geography coherent and yet permeable by promoting mutual knowledge and respect for the complex histories and current priorities of literary geography and its component disciplines. This would emphasise the strong human geography/literary studies interdisciplinarity of the field, which distinguishes it from somewhat related areas drawing to a degree on spatial theory and human geography but maintaining their disciplinary identity as literary criticism or literary studies. It would also disable attempts to create 'from X to Y' progress narratives for literary geography, not only because progress narratives imply that some approaches are past their use-by date, but also because the various permutations of interdisciplinary intersection are too complex to be represented as unidirectional.

3

GENRES

Over the past century literary geography's repertory of textual genres has expanded steadily, developing from an early focus on the regional novel and non-fictional descriptive writing to include a wider range of literary fiction and poetry, and then subsequently adding various genres of popular fiction, children's stories, graphic fiction and place writing. In addition, other forms and genres continue to be taken up by literary geographers as the field develops, including most recently testimony, folklore and 'real time' writing such as narratives broken up into Twitter-style posts. The subsections in this chapter follow a simple outline of basic genres, all of which could be thoroughly debated from a genre studies perspective, with the purpose being simply to provide a brief introduction to the generic range explored by work in literary geography since the late 1890s.

As a quick look at any one of the thematic sections of the online bibliography 'literary geographies' will show, there is a vast amount of work in the general area of literary/geographical studies which can be organised according to literary genre. The bibliography, however, like the online journal *Literary Geographies*, functions as an inclusive venue for a spectrum of work which includes, but also extends beyond, the more strictly delimited interdiscipline of literary geography. Taking a more targeted approach than the bibliography, this brief overview of work on the various genres with which literary geography has engaged concentrates on work which relates directly to literary genre and also to academic human geography, in many cases because it was published in a specialist geography journal, or because it frames its argument by reference to aims in human geography. This is both a practical limitation and an argument about the nature of the literary geography interdiscipline. Thinking pragmatically, it's clear that the vast range of work on literature/geography now being produced in different academic contexts and with different purposes would be beyond the scope of any attempt at a chapter-length thematic outline. Even more importantly, the limited number of examples in this chapter enables the focus on the human geography dimension to contemporary literary geography to be maintained, supporting the idea that the interdiscipline is not a matter of theme but of aims and academic context. Even a very brief overview of the genres of literary geography only becomes possible when the field is understood not as a loose collection of all kinds of work sharing a similar theme but as a coherent project with its roots in 20th-century human geography.

Genre has been a productive concept for literary geography in several ways. An awareness of the limitations of the field's existing repertoire of 'useful' genres has on several occasions inspired the field in new directions, and as the priorities and aims of literary geographers have shifted over time and in tune with developments in geography more generally, new genres have come into prominence. In addition, as Marc Brosseau has pointed out (2017), thinking about genre also highlights the importance of the author–reader collaborations fundamental to a spatial approach to the negotiation of meaning. Citing Tzvetan Todorov's work on genre, Brosseau points out that while a genre (such as 'crime fiction') provides an author with a writing model, to be followed or subverted, it also provides informed readers with a set of expectations which help structure their understanding and appreciation – or shape their resistance. Literary geography engages with the concept of genre for one more important reason: the priorities of literary geography having as much to do with 'geographical relevance' as 'literary merit', its repertoire of genres ranges particularly widely, from the more literary (for example, lyric poetry) to the more popular (such as detective fiction and comic books) even stretching to forms of creative writing which go beyond the scope of traditional genres (graffiti, for example, and sky writing).

REGIONALISM

Work on literary fiction and the geography of regions dates back further than a century, originally concentrating on 19th-century realism. As discussed in the previous chapter, the benefits and disadvantages of this early orientation towards realism and the regional novel have been the subject of considerable debate. Regions are both actual and imagined, geographical areas which supersede the local and form parts of the national or transnational. They are inseparably connected to the texts through which they are articulated and by which they are shaped. In the USA, regional literary geography was often associated with the short story and with local colour fiction, as for example in Elias Lieberman's *The American Short Story: A Study of the Influence of Locality in Its Development* (1912). The regional is not necessarily rural: Alison and Alistair McCleery's 'Personality of place in the urban regional novel' (1981), for example, reads George Blake's Glasgow novel *The Shipbuilders* to encourage the study of the urban regional novel in literary geography.

Focusing on Southern California, Dydia DeLyser's *Ramona Memories* (2005) records in detail the impact of the hugely popular novel *Ramona* (by Helen Hunt Jackson, 1884) in establishing its regional identity. Published just as new westbound railroad lines were enabling fans and tourists to visit the novel's fictionalised locations, *Ramona* had a dramatic effect on the region, and continues to attract tourists today: The Ramona Pageant has been performed annually to large audiences since 1923. DeLyser's *Ramona Memories*, like McLaughlin's 2016 work on American fans of the Sherlock Holmes stories discussed below, exemplifies the way in which work in literary geography is able to oscillate between the intra-textual and the extra-textual. This kind of literary geography connects the written geographies 'inside' the text and the literal geographies 'outside' the text, the swing between the two depending on what James Thurgill calls a 'spatial hinge' (Thurgill, 2021).

Over time the focus of regional literary geography has expanded to include poetry as well as fiction. Geographer John Tomaney has discussed Basil Bunting's mainly free verse long poem Briggflatts, for example, 'as an example of a narrative of regional identity' in *Environment and Planning D: Society and Space* (2007). Tomaney explains that 'Bunting's poetry demonstrates the progressive potential of regional narratives while avoiding recourse to a crude metaphysics of scale', adding that the poem develops a narrative of 'local and regional identity in ways which transcend the dichotomies with which social scientists in general, and geographers in particular, perennially struggle' (355). A later geographically-oriented reading of Bunting's work, Neal Alexander's 'The idea of north: Basil Bunting and regional modernism' (2013), emphasises the 'refraction' of the local and the regional through an international modernist poetics. Where Alexander's work on Bunting brings together regionalism and modernism, Juha Ridanpää's extensive work on literary geography and the idea of the region intersects with his interest in themes of humour, gender, metafiction and the postcolonial, as, for example, in articles such as 'A masculinist northern wilderness and the emancipatory potential of literary irony' (*Gender, Place and Culture*, 2010) and 'Dark humor, irony, and the collaborative narrativizations of regional belonging' (*GeoHumanities*, 2019).

MODERNIST FICTION

Despite the common idea that literary geographers have concentrated their attention on regional realism and avoided modernist texts, geographical work with literary modernism has a relatively long history. In addition to the articles published in the 1980s by J.D. Porteous, Brian Robinson's work has also emphasised the geographical significance of spatial fragmentation, as already mentioned. Marc Brosseau has argued that Robinson successfully demonstrated 'that literature does not "translate" a concrete experience directly and that there is not necessarily a unity in space but rather a spatiotemporal fragmentation', meaning that the 'modern' novel 'requires other reading practices'. In this way Robinson redirected 'geography's relationship with literature towards 'problems related to literary forms' (Brosseau, 1994: 348). Brosseau himself engaged with modernist fiction in his 1995 article 'The city in textual form: *Manhattan Transfer*'s New York', in which he argues that the novel 'represents, in its form as well as its content, the city in its socio-spatial complexity'. It gives the reader 'the opportunity to reflect on the interaction between a certain conception of the city and the formal aspects of the discourse used to represent it' (Brosseau, 1995: 93–94) As Brosseau had explained a year earlier in his review article, 'Geography's literature' (1994), *Manhattan Transfer* reveals 'how the interpretation of the city is not (only) expressed transitively but also embedded in the materiality of the text itself' (349). In the literary studies context of critical literary geography, Andrew Thacker (2005) called for studies to connect 'the external social space of the city with the internal spatial form of the text', as many modernist works 'not only depict societies in which space is being ferociously reconstituted, they also register in their own textual spaces the effects of urban modernization', a theme he tracked in his *Moving Through Modernity: Space and Geography in Modernism* (2003) and (with Peter Brooker) in *Geographies of Modernism* (2007).

POETRY

As Neal Alexander and David Cooper point out in their collection *Poetry & Geography: Space and Place in Post-War Poetry* (2013), work in literary geography has historically tended to concentrate on the novel. It is nevertheless possible to recuperate a scattered collection of academic work on poetry within human geography, often external to the UK tradition, while today the work of geographer-poets is becoming increasingly mainstream.

Historically, there is also an interesting history of interactions between poets and geographers, an early and significant example of which is the relationship between the Black Mountain poets and the geographer Carl Sauer, the poet Charles Olsen in particular having been inspired by Sauer's work on the cultural landscape, especially his 1925 *The Morphology of Landscape*.

Canadian poetry and its links to regionalism were the subject of work by J. Wreford Watson, who was himself (as James Watson) an award-winning poet, an early example of the now well-established academic/creative identity 'geographer-poet'. Watson's 1965 article for *The Geographical Journal* on 'Canadian regionalism in life and letters' includes detailed readings of poems by authors including E.J. Pratt, Tom Thompson and A.J.M. Smith. Slightly later, Audrey Kobayashi's 'Landscape and the poetic act: the role of haiku clubs for the Issei' (1980), is a very early engagement not only with the poetry of Japanese Canadians but also with themes that would later become significant to literary geography in general, especially to what has become known as relational literary geography. Kobayashi's work on haiku clubs considers the poems not only as art forms but also as artefacts reflecting, reproducing and documenting the experience of a very specific author/audience community: she focuses attention on haiku writing and sharing within this community as a collective articulation of group identity that was largely unrelated to assessments of literary value. Kobayashi continued her work with Japanese Canadian poetry in a book chapter on poetry and landscape for *A Few Acres of Snow: Literary and Artistic Images of Canada*, a significant 1992 anthology of work which also included E.M. Gibson's 'Theory in literary geography: the poetry of Charles Mair'.

Comparative literature scholar Martin Leer began publishing work on Australian poetry in the 1980s, writing on David Malouf, Randolph Stow and Les Murray, while Xiao-lun Wang published 'Geography and Chinese poetry' in the *Geographical Review* in 1990. In the 1990s, humanistic geography in South Africa looked at street poetry, with C.L. MacPhail emphasising the value of Soweto poetry and its powerful articulation of the black urban experience in an article on 'poetry and pass laws' for the *South African Geographical Journal* (1997). MacPhail draws attention to the question of whether poems or other texts need to be of 'literary merit' to be included in geographical research, again pointing out that poetry does not have to be critically endorsed in order to be of value. James Tyner, Sokvisal Kimsroy and Savina Sirikand (2015) took the study of poetry in literary geography in a different direction with an article for the *Annals of the American Association of Geographers* in which they considered poems produced by the Khmer Rouge 'as a form of public pedagogy' which presented 'nature as the fulcrum on which society was to be transformed'. As a result these poems can be viewed as 'representations of a landscape envisioned but not realized', 'pedagogic devices informing citizens of how life was to be lived, creative interventions with political purposes' (1285).

DRAMA

Work on geography and drama is often most interested in the geographic imagination and knowledge of a particular historical period, rather than in making texts and performances the subject of the kind of geographically oriented analysis typical of literary geography, and is in that sense often closer to historical geography. John Gillies' *Shakespeare and the Geography of Difference* (1994), for example, 'explores Shakespeare's geographic imagination', considering the 'intimate relationship between Renaissance geography and theatre'. Gillies offers a useful insight into the problems with terminology which beset contemporary literary geography in relation to definitions of 'literary cartography' and 'mapping' with his explanation that Shakespeare's images of the 'barbarous, outlandish or strange' (99) are grounded in literal cartographic practice, so that marginalisation was not only a matter of social status, but had to do with being literally positioned on the margins of contemporary maps. In discussing the connections linking maps and metaphors, Gillies also emphasises the similarities of the map and the theatre.

Shakespearean drama has also been explored by geographers working on historical and legal themes. John Wylie's 2000 article

'New and old worlds: *The Tempest* and early colonial discourse', for example, turns to *The Tempest* to consider links between colonial and geographical discourses. Wylie argues that colonial discourses and the colonization process can be understood as 'both emerging from, and relying upon, a series of European theological and classical understandings of the morality of voyaging, and the nature of the geographically distant' (45). Stuart Elden has written extensively on Shakespeare and the concept of territory, as for example in his 2013 article 'The geopolitics of *King Lear*: territory, land, earth' and his 2018 monograph *Shakespearean Territories*, in which he discusses what Shakespearean drama can reveal about territory as a political concept dependent on technological advantages in metrics, navigation, cartography and surveying.

At the literary studies end of the literary geographies spectrum, *The Cultural Geography of Early Modern Drama, 1620–1650* (Sanders, 2011) applies the work of cultural geographers to texts from the early modern period. As the publisher's summary online explains, Sanders focuses on 'forests, coastlines and arctic landscapes of ice and snow, as well as the more familiar locales of early modern country estates and city streets and spaces', taking geography as something 'kinetic, embodied and physical'. The Oxford University Press book series *Early Modern Literary Geographies* was launched shortly afterwards, in 2015. Also from 2011, and connecting literary analysis with work on time-space geography, Jonathan Bollen and Julie Holledge's 'Hidden dramas: cartographic revelations in the world of theatre studies' for *The Cartographic Journal* (2011), uses cartographic and network visualisations in its study of Ibsen's *A Doll's House*. Bollen and Holledge look at the production history of Ibsen's play in order to suggest the value of cartography to the field of theatre historiography.

While work on film has some obvious connections to work on drama within literary geography, film geography has been a separate field of enquiry in human geography since the early 1990s and an established subfield since the early 2000s. In their 2006 review of the field, Stuart Aitken and Deborah Dixon note that invigorated theoretical debates on the character of representation and meaning production have resulted in the development of both spatial ontologies of film and filmic ontologies of space. This theoretical sophistication offsets the narrow empiricism of earlier work, dispelling notions that geographers either naively embrace certain films as tools for representing geographic concepts (landscape, space, place and so forth) or they unabashedly borrow from film theory to help elaborate geographic questions.

(2006: 326)

PLACE WRITING

Established relatively recently as a named genre of creative writing, place writing aims to 'generate new knowledge' about 'place and human relationships with place', according to the online website for The Centre for Place Writing at Manchester Metropolitan University. David Cooper (2020) argues for an 'expansive understanding of place writing that incorporates the imagined geographies of fiction as well as the first-person accounts of geographical experience offered in creative non-fiction and lyric poetry', suggesting that place writing is a literary genre 'analogous to the similarly heterogeneous genre of life writing' (634). Some accounts of place writing emphasise the way in which it moves literary 'setting' and description of place and landscape from the background to the foreground, suggesting productive links both with the professional non-fictional writings on place produced over the last century by geographers and with the work of the geographer-poets. Within human geography, this kind of creative non-fiction has a long-standing history in professional debates about objectivity, accessibility and creativity in the writing styles of geographers.

CRIME, MYSTERY AND DETECTIVE FICTION

In one of the earliest geographical works to engage with this genre, Douglas McManis (1978) asked 'why geographers have ignored mystery fiction in their studies of literary landscapes' given that 'mystery writing is an abundant source of literary geography'. At the time McManis was writing, 'literary geography' had not yet become established as the field's collective term for geographical work with literary texts, and he uses 'literary geography' to describe an aspect of the text, referring to the subfield as geographical 'studies of literary landscapes'. Yi-Fu Tuan's 1985 article for the *Journal of Geography* on 'The landscapes of Sherlock Holmes' emphasises the complexity of their city settings, within which Holmes is uniquely qualified, physically as well as intellectually, to negotiate an urban space 'grown unmanageably large and complex', full of 'seething unassailable elements that might erupt in violence'. The detective is capable of dealing not only with the city but also with its far-reaching imperial connections: 'Holmes is almost never disoriented' (58). Twenty years after McManis was wondering why geographers had paid so little attention to mystery fiction, Lisa Kadonaga (1998) was still regretting that 'mystery novels and academic geography have not often intersected' despite the interestingly geographical ability of mysteries to 'incorporate spatial relationships and real-life regional characteristics' (24). Kadonaga argues that mystery writing had finally become 'freed from the long tradition of presenting elaborate puzzles', noting that by the late 1990s writers such as Ruth Rendell were featuring 'human interactions in realistic settings' and 'integrating place into their character development and plot lines' (24).

David McLaughlin's work on Conan Doyle's Sherlock Holmes stories looks at the ways in which Holmes fans extend their reading into their lived physical surroundings. His 2016 article 'The game's afoot: walking as practice in Sherlockian literary geographies', for example, discusses three late-20th-century examples of Holmes-related literary tourism in which the authors use 'the power of walking to combine embodied experience of the actual world with acts of memory and imagination' in order 'to inscribe the Sherlock Holmes texts into the world' in such a way that 'their walking and its representation become a form of both reading and writing, a physical experience of the unfolding of narrative in time and space' (2016: 144). Nicola Gabellieri is another geographer working on detective fiction: In her article for *GeoJournal* (2021) 'Place matters: geographical context, place belonging and the production of locality in Mediterranean

Noirs', Gabellieri contrasts the work of classic era detective writers with more recent works set in Europe. Gabellieri argues that these more modern stories allow readers 'to explore the writer's representation/construction of his own territorial context, or place-setting, which functions as a co-protagonist of the novel', also arguing that the greater role of place in popular crime fiction can be understood as a 'literary and geographical discourse aimed at the production of locality'.

In recent years crime and detective fiction has also stimulated work in literary cartography (defined in the literal sense). *The Cartographic Journal* published two articles on crime fiction in 2011, Eva Erdmann's 'Topographical fiction: a world map of international crime fiction' and Jennifer Jenkins's 'Out of place: geographical fiction(s) in Håkan Nesser's Inspector Van Veeteren series'. Pointing to 'the transformation of the genre from a literature of crime into a literature of geographical and cultural orientation', Erdmann proposed a 'crime fiction world map' in order to examine the international range of the genre and identify 'gaps and significant clusters', a project which would also form 'a collection of fictitious and narrative descriptions of localities' (2011: 274). Jenkins, meanwhile, concentrates on a series of novels with an invented fictional setting, the author's aim being 'a stripping of geographical connotation in order to create possibilities for readers to engage in their own poetic practice of image-creation – one neither based on nor burdened by geographical knowledge or accuracy'. Despite his efforts, some readers felt 'compelled towards acts of compensatory cartography that reflect a drive to establish an environmental orientation even within geographically indeterminate literary worlds'. Jenkins considers how these author/reader interactions 'initiate reflection on the nature of the relationship between fictional texts and the "real" world from which they simultaneously emerge and ontologically differ' (285).

Sally Bushell's article on 'The slipperiness of literary maps: critical cartography and literary cartography' (2012) employs detective fiction in a case study of maps included as components in fictional narratives, again connecting the crime fiction genre with work in literary cartography. The theoretical explorations of the first half of her article are subsequently worked out in critical practice in analyses of the use Agatha Christie makes of house plans in *The Mysterious Affair at Styles* and *The Murder of Roger Ackroyd*. Bushell also draws attention to the self-referentiality of the short story form in crime writing, suggesting interesting links with work on geography and metafiction (Ridanpää, 2010).

ADVENTURE FICTION

Work in literary geography on adventure fiction has historically had a significant crossover with studies of children's literature, as for example in the case of Richard Phillips's 'Politics of reading: decolonizing children's geographies', published in *Cultural Geographies* in 2001. Explaining that the politics of reading include both how and what people read, Phillips concentrates on the second question, looking at 'decolonizing' interventions into children's reading of adventure fiction in Britain in the 1970s. The following year, Garth Myers published 'Colonial geography and masculinity in Eric Dutton's *Kenya Mountain*' in *Gender, Place & Culture*, performing a close reading of the 1929 book as 'a contribution to critical feminist geographical understanding of colonial discourse'. Myers argues that 'Dutton's discursive tactics in the text reveal the inextricable relations between a gendered and enframed sense of landscape and colonial rule' (2002: 23).

'Space, setting, and the adventure story: or, With Perry in Japan', published in *Genre: Forms of Discourse and Culture* (Hones, 2006) uses spatial theories of distance to explore the way in which the popular 1903 novel *A Son of Satsuma* scripted the geography ('graphed the geo') of US–Japan relations at the turn of the 20th century. Arguing that the plot depends on 'the sudden implosion of apparent distance into productive proximity' the article proposes that while the novel is only partially set in Japan it is fully 'set' in an understanding of the world that was 'ready to see distance as relative and relational, and space as flexible':

> As a result, this is a narrative which not only implants a familiar story – 'orphan makes good' – in a distant location; it is at the same time a

narrative which implants a distant location – 'Japan' – in a familiar story. With its production of this reversible setting, the text folds literal distances into relational proximities in two directions: *A Son of Satsuma* is not only set in Japan; Japan is also set in *A Son of Satsuma*. The resulting reversibility, the sense that the fixed distances and geometric area of absolute space are being textually 'folded' in a conflation of genre and geography, is articulated in narrative details throughout the text.

(2006: 50)

CHILDREN'S FICTION

Children's literature has been a feature in literary geography since the early 20th century, primarily at first in relation to the stimulation of the geographical imagination in the geography classroom. Two of the many articles dealing with this intersection are 'Landscape and social values in children's literature: Nancy Drew mysteries' (Brooker-Gross, 1981) and 'Geography is children's literature, math, science, art and a whole world of activities' (Dowd, 1990), both published in *Journal of Geography*. Work on this genre at first tended to intersect with classroom practice, children's geographies, the adventure story and cartography, but later developments introduced it into urban geographies, geographies of nostalgia, the postcolonial and literary cartography (in the sense of literal mapping).

Focusing on the city-state of Singapore, Lily Kong and Lily Tay analysed the way in which it was depicted in local children's literature in their 1998 article for *Area*, 'Exalting the past: nostalgia and the construction of heritage in children's literature'. They argue that the stories are 'characterized by a nostalgic recollection of past times and places' and that nostalgia in general was so notable in Singapore because of the way in which the city has undergone 'phenomenal changes' within the lifespan of a single generation (1998: 133). Writing for *Children's Geographies* in 2006, Jenny Bavidge's 'Stories in space: the geographies of children's literature' investigates the extent to which children's stories coincide with their actual lived experiences of the city.

Working at the overlap of literary cartography and children's fiction, David Cooper and Gary Priestnall's 'The processual intertextuality of literary cartographies: critical and digital practices', published in *The Cartographic Journal* in 2011, explores the concept of 'processual intertextuality' in a case study of the maps reproduced within Arthur Ransome's *Swallows and Amazons* (1930) as well as reader-generated maps of the same story. Developing Kitchin and Dodge's work on processual cartography (discussed in the next chapter), Cooper and Priestnall's 'processual intertextuality' enabled them to think of literary maps as 'systems of cultural signification which are inextricably embedded within the material world and which are brought into being with each embodied reading or use' (2011: 250).

COLONIAL/POSTCOLONIAL LITERARY GEOGRAPHY

The postcolonial has emerged since the late 20th century as an important focus of work in literary geography, with work on texts often supporting reflection on the postcolonial in geography more generally. In their 1986 article on 'The Malay world in colonial fiction' Lily Kong and Victor R. Savage set out 'to reconstruct, as accurately as possible, the perceptions and attitudes of Westerners through an analysis of their spontaneous and candid fictional writings'. Kong and Savage focus first, on 'perceptions of the physical landscape (including elements such as climate, physical landforms, seas, rivers, vegetation, flora, fauna, and jungles)'; and second, on 'the cultural landscape (the population, the cultural life, and the physical landscape that has been transformed by human activities)' (1986: 40).

A particularly influential set of related articles have brought the methods of literary geography to the struggle within geography to establish a consciously postcolonial disciplinary practice. In 2008, Patricia Noxolo, Parvati Raghuram and Clare Madge published '"Geography is pregnant' and 'geography's milk is flowing": Metaphors for a postcolonial discipline?' in *Environment and Planning D: Society and Space.* Here the co-authors place their argument in the context of two overtly postcolonial fictional texts, applying metaphors of pregnancy and lactation to 'the imperatives arising from British academic geography's postcolonial position', emphasising the discipline's paradoxical struggle to be global while continuing to erase voices and perspectives from 'the margins' (146). Bringing this literary/postcolonial geography approach to a discussion of poetry as a geographical research method, Gabriel Eshun and Clare Madge's '"Now let me share this with you": exploring poetry as a method for postcolonial geography research' (*Antipode*, 2012) considers the 'possibilities and limitations of poetry as a means of re-representing and interpreting data collected through in-depth qualitative interviews', eventually reaching an ambivalent conclusion, not least because 'the representative qualities of poetry are never unproblematic or straightforward' and because academics 'are always complicit in the knowledge creation process' (1395). The following year, Patricia Noxolo and Marika Preziuso continued the combination of literary geography and work on the postcolonial with their article for *Annals of the Association of American Geographers* (2013) the 'Postcolonial imaginations: approaching a "fictionable" world through the novels of Maryse Condé and Wilson Harris'. Noxolo and Preziuso argue that engagement with postcolonial literature can form an important strategy in the push toward 'greater multivocality in geographical knowledge' called for by postcolonial geographers, focusing on the way in which literary texts produce the world as 'fictionable' in the sense of being 'open to multiple interpretations and perspectives'. Taking up the idea of the 'text as a spatial event' (Hones, 2008), 'in which writers, texts, and readers jointly create meaning', the article focuses on the fictions of Maryse Condé and Wilson Harris. It includes close readings of extracts from *La Colonie du Nouveau Monde* and *Jonestown* to show how the idea of the 'fictionable world' enables experiences 'of not only reading but of being read by the "other"' (163).

SCIENCE FICTION AND FANTASY

Work on science fiction and fantasy dates back to the 1970s, when it was often associated with the teaching of environmental issues. In their 1980 bibliographical essay for the *Journal of Geography*, 'Science fiction for geographers: selected works', Gary Elbow and Tom Martinson refer to an even earlier bibliography prepared for the Council of Planning Librarians by geographer William Rabiega (1974) on the use of science fiction as a guide to possible future environmental conditions. Lisa Kadonaga's article for *Western Geography* (1995) 'Novel landscapes: geographies of a future North America' starts from the premise that science fiction and speculative fantasy are frequently and usefully 'set in altered versions of real present-day landscapes' and that 'these fictional worlds reflect popular concerns about technology, social problems, and environmental change' (24). Geographical interest in science fiction was boosted by Rob Kitchin and James Kneale's 2001 article 'Science fiction or future fact? Exploring imaginative geographies of the new millennium', for *Progress in Human Geography*. Kitchin and Kneale used a critical reading of cyberfiction to 'look at fictional visions of postmodern urbanism in the early twenty-first century' and also at the ways in which cyberfictional strategies of 'estrangement and defamiliarization' and the 'destabilization of the foundational assumptions of modernism' provide 'a cognitive space in which to contemplate future spatialities' (19). The subsequent publication of their 2002 edited collection *Lost in Space: Geographies of Science Fiction* further consolidated the science fiction and fantasy genres within literary geography, also sustained by Kneale's later publications on H.P. Lovecraft (2006) and William Gibson (2011).

The connection between science fiction and environmental geography continues in work such as 'These overheating worlds', published in the *Annals of the American Association of Geographers* in 2014 by Kendra Strauss, which argues that 'the flourishing interest in narrative, stories, and storytelling in human geography opens up opportunities for exploring political imaginaries of climate change through utopian and dystopian impulses present in its "fictionable worlds"' (342). More recently, *Literary Geographies* 6 (1) included an editorial and several articles on science fiction in the theme section 'Critical worldbuilding: toward a geographical engagement with imagined worlds' (2020).

Fantasy fiction has also been part of literary geography since the 1970s, although Myles Balfe suggested in his article 'Incredible geographies? Orientalism and genre fantasy' for *Social and Cultural Geography* (2004) that despite its popularity 'the Fantasy genre has been largely ignored by academic geography'. Balfe set out to provide an 'overview of the genre, its politics and its geographies' and to argue that fantasy 'is not a transcendental and surpassing genre' working with purely imaginary spaces but is always implicated in real world discourse (75), arguing that 'the construction of the "Western" characters as the "good guys" in genre Fantasy texts can become problematic when these characters encounter "Other" peoples', and that the texts often 'confirm feelings of moral and cultural superiority when "we" encounter "them" in Fantasy narratives' (76).

GHOST STORIES AND TALES OF THE SUPERNATURAL

In the early 2000s, following a growing interest across the humanities in affect, memory and trauma, geographers began to apply the language of spectrality and haunting to their analyses of place and space, absence and presence. In 2008, a special issue of *Cultural Geographies* on 'spectro-geographies' linked the 'spectral turn' with literary geography by including an examination of the spectral landscapes of author Mary Butts (Matless, 2008). More recently, James Thurgill combined work on spectral geographies with the theoretical framework of the 'text as a spatial event' in his 'Extra-textual encounters: locating place in the text-as-event: an experiential reading of M.R. James' "A Warning to the Curious"' (2018). Thurgill reads short tales of the supernatural in the context of the actual-world landscape of the East Anglian landscape, 'weaving together ghostly narratives of the imagined with regional folklore, local history and topographical description' and exploring 'the particular affective qualities that are afforded by a narrative set within a landscape that is known to both author and reader, and where a performance of place can be seen to underpin the nature of the extra-textual encounter' (221).

SHORT STORIES

Short story forms have inspired several productive discussions in literary geography, including an exchange on the benefits and limitations of the compressed story format. In a 2008 article on the short fiction of Charles Bukowski, Marc Brosseau raised the question of whether the short story, as a genre, might not be inherently 'ageographical', given that it was unlikely to be able to provide literary geographers with the kind of material they tended to look for in the full-length novel, of 'the influence of space on character development, subject formation and social life more generally' (382). While acknowledging that the short story might be considered lacking in that sense, Brosseau argued that its strength lay in its use of generic settings that were able to function thematically. A response to Brosseau's article, which also engaged with a much earlier article by Yi-Fu Tuan on the geography of the Sherlock Holmes short stories, suggested that the shortness of the short story might actually be a practical benefit for literary geography, because it enables readers to engage directly and quickly with the primary material used by other scholars (Hones, 2010). This is important because, as Brosseau had pointed out earlier, work in literary geography depends upon detailed knowledge of and engagement with 'the literary text as text' (1994: 349). The 2010 article also took up Alice Walker's extremely short story 'Petunias' as a case study designed to illustrate the potential for literary geography of a radically short text with no clear setting or landscape description, arguing that the geographical point of the story was the way in which it asked readers 'to exercise a particular kind of spatial knowledge' (Hones, 2010: 479). The story 'uses disparate geographic references and a splintered narrative to encourage readers to participate in the connection of national and transnational spatial histories that have conventionally been separated' (479).

Another line of work on the short story considers full collections and story cycles from a geographical perspective. In a 1995 article on spatial and temporal dislocation in the South African short story cycle, Sue Marais argued that this kind of collection 'evinces a dualism which renders it particularly well suited to the representation of ... tension between centripetal and centrifugal or entropic impulses', and is as a result 'especially apposite to the South African context, where the conflict between community, solidarity and national unity, on the one hand, and dissociation, segregation and "apartheid," on the other, is notorious' (29).

More recently, approaching a short story collection from a cartographic perspective, Sara Luchetta has argued that collections offer the reader a significant agency, as they are able to choose whether to follow the published structure of the collection or read the stories in some alternative order, thereby generating 'unpredictable connections'. As a result, readers can 'make the collection happen in different ways, converting the short stories into tiles of a mobile mosaic', meaning that as a 'montage' which can be 'continually negotiated' the collection is 'not merely a material surface that can be freely read, but the theatre of the production of meanings'. In this way Luchetta looks at the ways in which short story collections can function as sites for 'the production of spatial meaning and knowledge' (Luchetta, 2018: 65).

GRAPHIC FICTION

Jason Dittmer's substantial series of articles on comic book geographies began in 2005 with 'Captain America's empire: reflections on identity, popular culture, and post-9/11 geopolitics'. While Dittmer's earlier work focused primarily on the comic book as a medium for the narration of national identity and popular geopolitics, his 2010 'Comic book visualities: a methodological manifesto on geography, montage and narration' provides an important general introduction to key themes for literary geographies of graphic fiction and comic books. Highlighting its material form, and offering the comic book as a corrective to the 'over focus on textual reading' in literary geography, Dittmer concentrates on the role of the reader in producing narrative, the distinction between a discursively produced audience and an actual readership, the microgeographies of page layout, conventions in reading and the ways in which the specifics of comic book visualities differ from the cinematic. Dittmer explains how the comic book 'requires the internalisation of a specific visuality involving the ability to translate the spatiality of two-dimensional sequential images into four-dimensional narrative' (222).

Another work on the literary geography of the comic book form from the mid-2000s is Juliet Fall's 'Embodied geographies, naturalised boundaries, and uncritical geopolitics in *La Frontière*

Invisible', published in *Environment and Planning D: Society and Space* (2006). Fall addresses questions of embodiment, spatiality and gender in a discussion of the representations of landscapes and of the female body in the two volumes of *La Frontière Invisible* (2002–2004), employing feminist geography and critical geopolitics in order to argue that the body, 'by posing an uncontrollable, unpredictable threat to regular ways of producing cartographic knowledge entails the possibility of a counter-strategic reinscription of spatial discourses and the creation of an alternative, more ethical cartography' (2006: 653). Situating graphic narrative not in relation to cartographic theory but to geopolitics, Edward Holland (2012) used Joe Sacco's *Chechen War, Chechen Women* to illustrate how popular geopolitical understandings come into being, arguing that 'oppositional formats, and graphic narratives in particular, challenge hegemonic scriptings of geopolitics through a bricolage of narrative techniques'. Holland shows how three narrative techniques Sacco employs, 'historical interlude, the singular panel, and the depiction of the banal', enable readers to grasp 'the individual, localised consequences of the Chechen conflicts' (105).

Giada Peterle, author of *Comics as a Research Practice: Drawing Narrative Geographies Beyond the Frame* (2021), has also linked the genre with cartography, both in the classroom and beyond, as in her 2015 article 'Teaching cartography with comics: some examples from BeccoGiallo's graphic novel series' and her 2016 article for *Cultural Geographies* on 'Comic book cartographies: a cartocentred reading of *City of Glass*, the graphic novel'. In his 2018 article for *Literary Geographies*, Maxwell Woods made the argument that Josh Neufeld's *AD: New Orleans After the Deluge*, which depicts the experiences of six New Orleans residents, 'represents the emerging geography of climate change as one in which a white, monied world is spared the forces of the Anthropocene and made the de facto center of power' (84). Finally, Stefan Ekman brought together fantasy and literary mapping in his *Literary Geographies* article 'Map and text: world-architecture and the case of Miéville's *Perdido Street Station*' (2018). Focusing on world-building and fantasy maps, Ekman argues that 'analysing a fantasy novel that comes with a map without taking into account the dynamic between map and text would be to omit a vital part of the fictional world' (66).

NEW FORMS

In recent years, literary geography has taken an interest in newer genres such as 'cli-fi' (climate fiction) as well as less conventional forms of writing, stretching the concept of textual genre as it functions within the interdiscipline. The literary geography of graffiti writing, for example, was the subject of Evan Carver's 2018 article for *Literary Geographies*, 'Graffiti writing as urban narrative'. Carver focuses on 'the interplay between text and context' as the graffiti site emerges as a narrative space, arguing that this approach not only complicates

> the traditional categorizations of what is 'literary' and what is 'geographic,' [but also] shows how a multi-authored text written directly onto the surfaces of the city can adaptively articulate social identity, resist powers that would inscribe a single legibility on urban space, and allow citizens to recognize the power – and responsibility – that comes with co-creating public space.
>
> (188)

Zachary Horton's 'Written on the sky: inscription, scale, and agency in anthropocenic semiotics' (2019) brings sky writing into literary geography, exploring 'the sky as a surface of inscription' with a study of David Antin's 1987–88 diptych 'Sky Poems', which were printed on, in or against the sky over a period of several hours. Horton argues that instead of 'attempting to scale-down the atmosphere's signs, David Antin's works point the way toward a scaling-up of human subjectivity toward collective and discontinuous forms of reading' which could 'close the circuit between species-scale writing and elemental reading' (2019: 54).

Finally, David Cooper has combined a discussion of contemporary place writing's 'phenomenological concern with the materiality of both the authorial self and the landscapes through which that body moves' in a consideration of 'place, the practice of everyday life, and the smartphone' in a range of non-fiction prose texts (2019, 90). In the first half of the article, Cooper considers the literary representation of digital technologies. Then he introduces the sub-genre of the geo-memoir and explores some key writings in which smartphones are framed as problematically distancing the self from place. Next, he goes on to consider the ways in which place is 'co-constituted through a knotty entangling of the material and the digital', and to propose a typology of the ways in which contemporary place writers use Twitter. The final section of the article examines

> how the Cumbrian shepherd, James Rebanks (*The Shepherd's Life*, 2015), has used Twitter, accessed via his smartphone, to document the quotidian experience of being-in-place. Ultimately, then, this article is interested in a core literary geographical question: how have recent creative non-fiction writers integrated the smartphone within a wider re-enchanting of the places and rhythms of everyday life?
>
> (2019: 107)

4
MAPPINGS

TERMINOLOGY

Maps, mapping and cartography have become increasingly important themes in literary geography in the 21st century for two main reasons. The first has to do with terminology and interdisciplinary communication: confusingly, terms like 'mapping' and 'literary cartography' tend to be used literally in human geography and metaphorically in literary studies. This difference easily leads to miscommunication and confusion. The second reason has to do with the increasing availability and sophistication of computer-mediated and digital mapping technologies. Although various modes of literary mapping have been important to work in literary geography since its earliest beginnings, new technologies are now revitalising academic literary cartography and at the same time making literary maps and mappings newly accessible and useful for the general public. One of the side effects of progress in mapping technologies and in cartographic theory has been that the gap between non-specialist uses of map-related terminology and the definitions used (and debated) in fields such as human geography has widened. This has led in turn to a gap opening up between the use of map terminology in literary geography and in literary studies, because for literary geographers 'mapping' typically refers (literally) to the process of making a graphic map, while in literary studies the same term is more often used metaphorically, to describe an aspect of written narrative or criticism. For example, in literary studies an article on 'mapping modernism' might suggest the metaphorical 'mapping' performed by a work of modernist fiction, or it might allude to a critical overview of literary modernism. In literary geography, the same title would be more likely to refer to a study of modernism which literally produced and used sets of maps. The problem is that while literal definitions seem natural to one group of readers, metaphorical usages seem equally obvious to another.

Paradoxically, because the new interest in spatial and geographical themes which started to take hold in literary studies in the 1990s coincided with the rapid development of map technologies in human geography, mutual understanding and communication between the two fields became even more difficult. 'Literary cartography' also splits into metaphorical and literal usages. In literary studies, literary cartography often refers to the ways in which literary texts themselves metaphorically 'map' space; in a more geographical context, the same term is more likely to refer to the actual processes of literary mapping, originally featuring hand-drawn maps and now more likely to involve computer-assisted mapping and cartographic software tools (GIS). In the first (metaphorical) instance, the author is understood to be the cartographer; in the second (literal) instance, the scholar who creates and uses maps to analyse literary material and its extra-textual geographies is the cartographer.

In much the same sense that for geographers 'spatial metaphors are problematic in so far as they presume that space is not', map-related metaphors are a problem for literary geographers because they depend on the assumption that terms and concepts such as 'map' and 'cartography' are self-evident. But for specialists they are not self-evident at all, and in fact are subject to constant reflection, discussion and adjustment. As David Cooper and Ian Gregory point out in their 2011 article on 'Mapping the English Lake District: a literary GIS', in the early 21st century 'mapping' has provided literary critics with a 'helpfully malleable metaphor':

> A by-product of this semantic pliability, however, is that the endlessly recycled metaphor has been stripped of geographical meaning and the mapping of a literary text has too often become elided with the process of critical practice. In other words, 'mapping', in literary studies, has frequently become synonymous with a way of reading.
>
> (91)

Whether 'mapping' terminology is used metaphorically or literally tends to depend on the user's position in regard to academic work in geography and cartography. For scholars working at a distance from specialist geographical fields, 'mapping' can easily be used in its everyday sense, the meaning of the term apparently obvious enough to provide the reliably stable half (the 'vehicle') of the metaphor. In contrast, for scholars engaged with theory and practice in geography and cartography, the mapping metaphors commonly used in literary studies have to be rethought, in non-specialist terms, in order to be recognised as references to presumably self-evident objects and practices. In other words, in order to make sense of the way the terms are used metaphorically in other academic fields, literary geographers have to put their academic experience on hold and translate those map-related terms and concepts into non-specialist language.

'Cognitive mapping' is a third term which generates gaps and misunderstandings in academic work on literary texts, not so much because it is used metaphorically but because it is commonly used in two very different senses, which have different meanings and implications. Both variants can be traced back to urban planner Kevin Lynch's *The Image of the City* (1960), in which he argues that in 'the process of way-finding, the strategic link is the environmental image, the generalized mental picture of the exterior physical world that is held by an individual' (5). In this original sense, 'cognitive mapping' refers primarily to literal way-finding, spatial orientation and spatial behaviour. An additional and more recent usage refers to Fredric Jameson's 'aesthetic of cognitive mapping' (Jameson, 1984), which he envisioned as a rethinking of 'specialized geographical and cartographical issues in terms of social space', and which deals with, for example, 'the ways in which we all necessarily also cognitively map our individual social relationship to local, national and international class realities' – the 'also' here presumably referring back to Lynch – and attempt to grasp 'global multinational and decentered communicational networks' (44). Here the way-finding is much less literal and the 'mental picture' quite different, and the point that Jameson's version is a 'rethinking' of 'specialized geographical and cartographical issues' is usually overlooked. Although the terminological difficulties associated with 'cognitive mapping' are less obvious than with the very different metaphorical and literal uses of a term like 'mapping', it is nonetheless helpful when using the term 'cognitive mapping' to be clear about category and scale.

NON-METAPHORICAL MAPS AND MAPPINGS IN LITERARY GEOGRAPHY

In the context of literary geography, terms such as 'maps', 'cartography' and 'cognitive mapping' are most commonly used in a straightforwardly literal sense to refer to theory and practice in cartography and human geography. 'Literal' literary maps can be divided into two main categories. The first is the map embedded in or attached to the text, either author-generated or added to the text prior to publication. The other is the reader-generated map produced post-publication, which could be a non-scholarly reader/fan map, or the work of an academic literary cartographer. While 'map' (as a noun) usually refers to the graphic object, 'mapping' emphasises not only the maps themselves but also the processes involved in their production, both in the sense that they are produced by a mapmaker, and also, more recently, in the sense that maps are 'produced' in the course of various linked processes involving map users as well as mapmakers. The first view, of maps as representations, enabled the work of geographer J.B. Harley (1988), who challenged the idea that cartographic representations could ever be entirely objective, thereby leading to the development of the field now known as critical cartography. The second, an 'ontogenetic' view of 'mapping' sometimes called 'post-representational mapping', depends on the idea that maps are not fixed representations but are unstable objects always in process, coming into being in the interplay of cartographer, map, and map user (Kitchin and Dodge, 2007).

MAPPING IN LITERARY GEOGRAPHY BEFORE THE 1970S

Although historiographical reviews of work on mapping and cartography in literary geography typically mention a few works from the late 19th and early 20th centuries and then skip forward to the 1980s, the period in between is far from empty. The earliest citations provided in literary geography reviews tend to be for thematic maps produced for the general reader and for literary tourists, such as those included in J.A. Erskine Stuart's *The Brontë Country: Its Topography, Antiquities, and History* of 1888 and *The Literary Shrines of Yorkshire* of 1892. An extensive bibliography of similar works in US and British literature is provided in Edith J. Roswell Hawley's 'Bibliography of Literary Geography' (1915–19) mentioned in Chapter 2. These are followed by broader scale surveys aimed at students of English literature such as William L. Phelps's 'A literary map of England' of 1899, and J. G. Bartholomew's 1910 *A Literary and Historical Atlas of Europe*.

The beginnings of analytical literary cartography, meanwhile, can be traced back to early 20th century German works such as S.R. Nagel's *Deutscher Literaturatlas* of 1907 and Josef Nadler's 1912 *Literaturgeschichte der Deutschen Stämme und Landschaften*. Nagel's atlas of literary Germany used thematic maps to make explanatory connections between geographical features and the biographies and works of various authors, also noting historical shifts in the spatial distribution of intellectual clusters. Having referred to these or similar early works, brief reviews of literary cartography tend to move on quickly from Nagel's positivist 'science of literary geography' to the 1980s, when the spatial turn in literary studies and the beginnings of computer-assisted mapping techniques came together to generate a new enthusiasm for literary mapping.

There is nonetheless some interesting activity in the use of maps within geographical work on literary texts in the gap between 1910 and 1980, including scholarly works in which authors included explanatory maps as part of their discussion and works dealing with authorial maps included within works of fiction. Early examples of the first category can be found in the essays J.K. Wright contributed to *The Geographical Review* between 1924 and 1938. In his essay on 'Geography in literature' (1924), for example, he supported his argument with a US map of 'local color regions' taken from R.L. Ramsay's *Short Stories of America* (1921). H.C. Darby's well-known article on Hardy's Wessex (1948) also uses maps to make its argument, in this case simplified maps of locations and drainage, geology, relief and main regions of Dorset, apparently hand-drawn by the author. J. Wreford Watson's 'Canadian regionalism in life and letters' (*Geographical Journal*, 1965), mentioned earlier as an example of work in literary geography on poetry and the region, also includes a hand-drawn map of 'Factors in Canadian regionalism'.

MAKING MAPS, PROVIDING INFORMATION

Work on maps, mappings and cartography in literary geography has a rather complex relationship to the broader history of cartography within human geography. In the very early stages of academic literary geography, cartography was a required geographical skill – technical but not greatly theorised – and its inclusion in work on literary texts was unremarkable. Later, as the geographical mainstream began to emphasise quantitative methods and the subfield of 'literature and geography' became marginalised, the use of illustrative maps in literary geography declined somewhat. Later still, with the development of computer-mediated mapping, the geoweb, GIS and mixed quantitative/qualitative methods, cartography in literary geography became reattached to the mainstream, both practically and in terms of theory. This can be seen in the emergence of a broadly 'post-representational' theory of cartography as process and the proposal within literary geography that literary texts 'happen' in temporo-spatial interactions, in that case more often identified as 'more-than-representational'. A useful guide to the geographical context for literary geography's map-related practices in the period from the mid-1970s until 2014 can be found in Rob Kitchin's overview article 'From mathematical to post-representational understandings of cartography: forty years of mapping theory and praxis in *Progress in Human Geography*' (2014). This provides a compact summary of 36 articles dealing specifically with cartography that were published in *Progress* between 1974 and 2014, some of them 'progress reports' and others general articles.

The earliest *Progress* reports are relevant to literary geography mainly because they indicate the gap between what was happening in literary geography at the time and the mainstream assumption that scientific and quantitative methods could provide solid explanations of geographical processes and systems. The difference between 'experience' and 'explanation' in human geography in the 1970s and 80s created a sharp split between early literary geography and the geographical mainstream. In accordance with the social science emphasis on explanation, the *Progress* articles from 1972 and 1974 view maps not simply as research outputs but also as data which could be entered into explanatory spatial models. Generally, in the mid-1970s, work on cartography in human geography was focusing on two main questions: how best to make maps, and maps as sources of information.

Meanwhile, work in literary geography on maps and mapping had quite different concerns. In their article 'Maps in literature', which appeared in *Geographical Review* in 1974, Phillip and Juliana Muehrcke valued the creative perspective, arguing that while the professional cartographer had to be concerned with the technical aspects of map production, 'the popular writer' was free to take a more 'philosophical and imaginative' approach. Arguing that 'as many writers point out, the very fact that a map does not reproduce reality is its great allure' (317), the Muehrckes maintain that 'a map can never be more than the elaborate fictions of cartographic methodology', and that what a cartographer might identify as 'the most serious limitations of a map' can, for literary geographers, become 'its greatest assets' (338, 337). This article marked the beginning of literary geography's engagement with maps included in literary texts, as opposed to articles in which geographers used or created maps to illustrate or support their argument.

Where the Muerhckes provide an early example of work in literary geography explicitly dealing with literary maps, Leslie Jay's 'The Black Country of Francis Brett Young', published in *Transactions of the Institute of British Geographers* the following year, follows the examples of Wright, Darby and Wreford Watson in using maps to support and illustrate his geographically-oriented reading of literary texts. Focusing on the idea of the urban region, Jay suggests that there are two kinds of 'regional consciousness': one which 'is observed and measured from outside the region'; and another which 'is experienced by the people living within it' (57). The qualitative/quantitative split becomes a factor here when Jay argues that a regional consciousness 'observed and measured from outside' can be dealt with by geographers making 'a scientific appraisal of the elements' which give the region its distinctive appearance, the second, experienced by inhabitants, 'is more difficult to assess objectively' and in that case 'the regional novelist often proves to be more successful than the geographer' (57).

MAPS AS COMMUNICATION SYSTEMS

The 1977 *Progress* report indicated a shift in the mainstream geographical view of cartography and mapping, in its discussion of Arthur Robinson and Barbara Petchenik's recently published *The Nature of Maps* (1976). This report inserted a new but fundamental question into a field concentrating at the time on practical issues of map production and maps as sources of information: what *is* a map? As Kitchin points out, the question of how best to define 'maps' and 'mapping' is still being debated today, with the idea that maps can usefully be thought of as processes rather than objects significantly complicating the issue. Not yet thinking in those terms, the 1977 review highlights Robinson and Petchenik's proposition that a map is 'a communication system designed to convey spatial relationships'. The penultimate article from the 1970s nonetheless returned to techniques of map reading and the potential of behavioural geography in analysing map use, while the final review focused on 'human factors in map design' (Kitchin, 2014: 2).

In the same year that the report in *Progress* reviewing Robinson and Petchenik's *The Nature of Maps* was published, geographer Charles Aiken published the first in his series of works on William Faulkner's fictional geographies, which culminated in 2009 with his monograph *William Faulkner and the Southern Landscape*. In 'Faulkner's Yoknapatawpha County: geographical fact into fiction', Aiken includes maps and photographs of the historical Oxford and Lafayette County as well as maps of the fictional Yoknapatawpha, the latter including a composite map developed from Faulkner's own hand-drawn maps for the novel *Absalom, Absalom!* and the extracts and short stories included in *The Portable Faulkner*. Advancing the literary geography tradition of exploring the ways in which fiction combines elements of the historical and the fictional, Aiken analyses in detail the process by which Faulkner's narrative world was created. Where Robinson and Petchenik's understanding of a map as 'a communication system designed to convey spatial relationships' describes the work performed by a standard geographical map, Aiken's use of various kinds of maps in his work on Faulkner's historical/fictional world reveals the more complicated set of temporo-spatial relationships which generate literary space.

GEOGRAPHIC INFORMATION SYSTEMS AND CRITICAL CARTOGRAPHY

The first of the two reports published in *Progress* in 1982 covered a wide range of topics, including teaching mapwork, mental maps, map reading, and the emerging technologies of computer-assisted cartography. Arguing in the second report from 1982 that the promise of the 'communication paradigm' had not been fulfilled, Mark Monmonier turned to a pragmatic rather than conceptual consideration of early forms of GIS, which although not yet publicly accessible through the geoweb were becoming increasingly important. The emphasis on cartography and GIS continued through reports and articles published in the 1980s and early 1990s, which also included discussions of the gap opening up between academic cartography and everyday map-making and map-using. Early critiques of GIS began to appear, at first focusing on its implicit positivism and the need for better theorisation. Although the acronym GIS is frequently used in references to map-making software and studies, and critiques of the design and use of that software, the two can also be formally distinguished as GISys (Geographic Information Systems) and GISci (Geographic Information Science). GIsys refers to computer software tools which enable mapping processes, while GIsci refers to studies of the social and political implications of those tools and the critique of associated processes of knowledge production. As a result, 'critical GIS' usually implies work affiliated with Geographic Information Science.

In the 1980s, when software tools for mapmaking were an important topic in human geography in general, literary geography was not yet making much use of GIS. The enduring theme of the ways in which map use in fiction might stimulate interest in the geography classroom was taken up again in 1985 in L.S. Levstik's 'Literary geography and mapping', which appeared in *Social Education*, while Adele Haft's 'The poet and the map: (di)versifying the teaching of geography' (1999) was the first of two linked papers which also provide good examples of this sustained tradition of work at the intersection of literary geography and geography teaching. Focusing on four 20th-century poets who write about maps, Haft suggests that since 'their poems have much to teach regarding the meanings and uses of maps' teachers could 'introduce students to their verses and apply their ideas to (di)versify the way we teach about maps and geography' (33).

By the 1990s Brian Harley's 'critical cartography', with its challenge to the idea that maps provided objective representations, was beginning to make a broad impact. Inspired by Derrida and Foucault, Harley saw deconstruction as the key to understanding the ways in which maps work and the complexities of their implication in systems of power. This ran directly counter to the idea still being expressed in cartography articles in *Progress* in 1994 that well-made maps are 'monosemic and non-ambiguous' (Kitchin, 2014: 3). In time, Harley's work led to a recognition of maps as social constructions and practices, and the development of 'post-representational' cartography (Kitchin and Dodge, 2007). Harley's influence on mapping in literary geography, and the impact of critical cartography in general, has been extensive: Sally Bushell's 'The slipperiness of literary maps: critical cartography and literary cartography' (*Cartographica*, 2012), for example, drew on critical cartography

> to define core concerns for an emerging literary cartography, such as the nature of the analogy between map and text; the complexity of correspondence when a map and text occur alongside each other and the author is also the map-maker; and the difficulties created by naïve users of the literary map.
>
> (149)

POST-REPRESENTATIONAL CARTOGRAPHY

Two other important works on cartography which would have a significant impact on literary geography more generally appeared in *Progress* in the early 2000s. According to Kitchin's review, Del Casino and Hanna's 'Representations and identities in tourism map spaces' (2001), was one 'of the first papers to argue explicitly for a post-representational cartography that understood maps as ongoing processes rather than representational products' (Kitchin, 2014: 4). Arguing that 'the moment of map production is no longer determinant', Del Casino and Hanna emphasised the way in which 'space, identities and maps' were being 'co-created through their use', that 'mapping is intertextual and contextual and meanings are never fixed'. They argued that critical cartography 'requires more than simply deconstructing their creation and associated power dynamics' extending to a consideration of 'how they are used in practice (Kitchin, 2014: 4)'. The following year, Jeremy Crampton's 'Maps as social constructions: power, communication and visualization', extended Harley's work in order to explore further the gap between thinking of 'maps as communication systems', on the one hand, and 'as sites of power-knowledge' on the other (Kitchin, 2014: 4). Kitchin points out that Crampton, like Del Casino and Hanna, created new ways of thinking about maps by employing ideas imported from critical human geography and social theory, while also emphasising the potential of looking at the role of the map-user as a participant in the cartographic process. These ideas were later absorbed into literary geography theory, both directly and also indirectly, through the work of Kitchin and Dodge (2007), feeding in to the development of the idea that – like maps – texts are 'intertextual and contextual' and 'meanings are never fixed'. In this way, cartographic theory and work on relational geography more broadly encouraged the emergence of the idea of the 'text as a spatial event' (Hones, 2008) and what would subsequently become known as 'relational literary geography' (McLaughlin, 2016).

In the 2000s a range of new concerns surfaced in *Progress* reports and articles: the 2002 report, for example, considered the potential of tactile mapping for visually impaired users, while the 2003 review reconsidered the disciplinary position of maps in human geography, arguing that work on maps fell into two groups: in the first, under the influence of the cultural turn, maps had essentially disappeared as analytic tools but were instead becoming increasingly subject to critical analysis and deconstruction themselves; in the second, maps were being treated as technical communication devices, with research focusing on how they worked in practice. Review articles in the mid-2000s dealt with more practical aspects of cartography, including map projections, cartographic uncertainty, public policy, and cybercartography. At the same time, interventions from feminist and gender geography into GIS theory and practice continued to build on the critiques and debates of the 1990s. The potential of a feminist-inspired GIS practice was Mei-Po Kwan's subject in a 2002 article for *Gender, Place and Culture* in which she argued that feminist practice would make it possible to 'open up new discursive spaces for subverting dominant GIS practices' and thereby to recast the 'oppositional debates' which had characterised earlier feminist critiques of GIS. This would be achieved by disrupting the rigid distinction between quantitative and qualitative methods in geographic research, acknowledging both 'the critical agency and subjectivities of the GIS user/researcher', and exploring 'the possibility for GIS to be practiced in a more reflexive manner' (271). As indicated by the increase in literary GIS projects and publications in recent years, the integration of quantitative and qualitative methods enabled by this kind of disruption is now standard practice, at least in literary cartography. The editors' introduction to the collection *Literary Mapping in the Digital Age* (Cooper et al., 2016), for example, emphasises that the book deals with the relationship of mapping practices, the application of geospatial technologies, and the interpretation of literary texts.

In the mid-2000s, at a time when GIS was only just starting to take hold as a method in literary geography, work on more traditional forms of literary cartography continued at its normal steady pace, for example in Adele Haft's substantial series of articles on poetry and cartography for *Cartographic Perspectives* (2000–15), which included work on Marianne Moore, Elizabeth Bishop, Kenneth Slessor and others. In 2003, Christina Ljungberg considered the question of how maps might help novelists negotiate the jump from 'reality to representation' because of the way in which they rendered more visible the gap between object and sign. Working with three novels which featured embedded maps, Ljungberg considered what maps 'make visible' when embedded in fiction, a line of thinking taken up by Sally Bushell in 2012 when she posited her three core questions about maps in fiction: what does the map add to the text?; what effect does reading the map have on reading the text, and vice versa?; and what do the map and the text reveal about each other? Bushell subsequently expanded her work on these questions and literary cartography in general in *Reading and Mapping Fiction: Spatialising the Literary Text* (2020).

MAPPING AS PROCESS

In their influential article 'Rethinking maps' (*Progress*, 2007) Kitchin and Dodge 'made the case for rethinking cartography as a processual, rather than representational, science' (331). Kitchin's own summary, taken from his 2014 review article, explains that they

> put forward the notion that it was productive to conceive of cartography as ontogenetic, that is, always in the process of making place.

> Drawing on the concepts of transduction and technicity, they contended that maps are of-the-moment, brought into being through practices (embodied, social, technical); that maps are never fully formed and their work is never complete – they are always mappings, that is, spatial practices enacted to solve relational problems (e.g. how best to create a spatial representation, how to understand a spatial distribution, how to get between A and B, and so on). Such an ontological reworking, they argued, opened the way for a new epistemology that focused on how maps were created and used in practice, rather than being fixated on the technical rules of production and politics of the artefact.
>
> (Kitchen, 2014: 5)

At around the same time that Kitchin and Dodge were generating the new more-than-representational approach to mapping which would encourage similar studies of narrative fiction in literary geography, Margaret Wicke Pearce's 'Framing the days: place and narrative in cartography' (2008) reversed standard practice by bringing narrative into mapping, rather than the other way around. Starting from the point that one of the themes of critical cartography 'is the question of how to map space as it is experienced', Pearce argued that the conventions of Western cartography lean toward to the expression of 'spaces of homogeneity and modernity, not the spaces shaped by human experience'. Pearce proposed adding narrativity to cartography to address this issue, using a historical map project as a case study (17).

GEOGRAPHIC INFORMATION SYSTEMS AND LITERARY CARTOGRAPHY

In 2009 the first of a series of articles on the use of GIS in literary geography by Iain Gregory and David Cooper appeared in the *International Journal of Humanities and Arts Computing*: 'Thomas Gray, Samuel Taylor Coleridge and Geographical Information Systems: a literary GIS of two Lake District tours'. Considering the potential of GIS for the humanities, Cooper and Gregory argue that two issues need to be confronted:

> first, that it is technically possible to create a useful GIS of textual material, the main medium through which humanities research is conducted; and, secondly that such a database can be used to enhance our understanding of disciplines within the humanities.
>
> (2009: 61)

The authors use as their case study a pilot study then underway at the University of Lancaster, which had created a GIS of two textual accounts of tours of the Lake District: Thomas Gray's (1769) and Samuel Taylor Coleridge's (1802). They argue that this pilot study showed it is both possible and productive 'to move GIS beyond the quantitative arena in which it currently resides and into more qualitative areas of humanities research' (61).

In the same year, Jeremy Crampton's two reports for *Progress* provide an overview of technological developments in online mapping, and a discussion of related cartographic theory. The first focuses on the increasing interactivity of maps, as they became more 'social and open in their creation through the crowdsourcing of cartographic information and use of open source licensing, but also in their use through geocollaboration, sharing and commenting' (Kitchin, 2014: 5). Kitchin summarises Crampton's second 2009 report as dealing with maps as 'performative, participatory and political', looking at the ways in which cartography was meeting up with art and psychogeography as well as 'forms of protest and political participation' (5). Crampton's third report (2011) considered the ways in which, in contrast, cartography can become 'enrolled' in 'political manoeuvres to claim, survey and police people and places'. In the same year as Crampton's earlier two reports (2009), Anders Sundnes Løvlie published an article in the *Journal of Location Based Services* in which he described the development of Textopia, an experimental 'locative literary system'. The 'locating reading' project was a practical experiment in a literary geography version of the participatory trend, which enabled users in an urban setting to listen to literary texts about the places in which they were at that moment located, and also to write and share their own place-related texts. He explains the practical process of designing a system prototype, early outcomes from user experiences and flaws in the system, and suggests directions for future development.

GAZETTEERS AND ONLINE MAPPING PROJECTS

With the increase in work on participatory and public mappings and websites, literary mapping began to return to the themes which had originally made gazetteers and atlases for both travelling and armchair literary tourists so popular. These kinds of guides to places associated with authors and literary works date back for centuries, forming a major part of the 'uncritical' literary geography aimed at the general public to which Thacker was reacting in his 'Idea of a critical literary geography' (2005). Three well-known works which built in different ways on this popular tradition in the late 20th century were Margaret Drabble and Jorge Lewinski's *A Writer's Britain: Landscape in Literature* (1979), David Daiches and John Flower's *Literary Landscapes of the British Isles: A Narrative Atlas* (1979), and Malcolm Bradbury's *Atlas of Literature* (1996). More details about works of this kind can be found in 'Mapping literary Britain: tourist guides to literary landscapes 1951–2007' (Philips, 2011) which analyses a range of guidebooks. This form of popular literary geography, aimed at a broad reading public, connects with the development of the multiple online literary GIS projects which were launched in the early 20th century, many of them directed towards both public engagement and scholarly research, which brought together theoretical work and freely available resources in their publications and websites.

Sara Luchetta's 2017 article for *Geography Compass*, 'Exploring the literary map: an analytical review of online literary mapping projects', reviews digital literary mapping projects 'where cartographic representations are produced by readers as analytical tools and/or as reading practices for literary texts' (e12303). Luchetta focuses on three processes or elements: the way projects process data collection; the tools used to map texts; and the project developers. URLs for online literary atlas/mapping projects can usually be found without difficulty using online search engines. Some examples both completed and under development are The Cultural Atlas of Australia; the Digital Literary Atlas of Ireland, 1922–1949; the Grub Street Project (mapping the geography of early modern London's literature and publishing);

Mapping Petersburg, Placing Literature (crowdsourcing 'literary locations'); a project on the spaces of Slovenian Literary Culture and another on the literature of Vilnia (Lithuania), among many others. The Literary Atlas for English language novels set in Wales is an interactive online atlas offering a range of 'variations on mapping', including one which locates all the 'blue plaques' commemorating links between geographical sites and famous Welsh writers. Linking to project co-leader Jon Anderson's *Page and Place: Ongoing Compositions of Plot* (2014), the atlas works with multiple connotations of the word 'plot'. The website explains that the project's variety of maps locate 'all geographical references (or "plotpoints") in twelve English-language novels primarily set in Wales'.

Positioned at the intersection of literary geography, GIS and the digital humanities, a series of projects at Lancaster University have also generated research output in the form of both scholarly publications and online open-access resources. Between 2007 and 2008 the project series started with a pilot study exploring the potential of using GIS to map historical accounts of the English Lake District. The five year Spatial Humanities project 'Texts, GIS and Places' (2012–16) then further developed this line of work, which since 2016 has continued as part of Lancaster University's Digital Humanities Hub. Among the many publications generated by this work at Lancaster University, the edited collection *Literary Mapping in the Digital Age* (Cooper et al., 2016) contains a wide range of chapters on different aspects of the book's theme, including for example the mapping of place names and of emotions as well as 'literary virtual geographies'.

While much of the work on literary geography and GIS has been achieved in mid- to large-scale collaborative research projects, individual literary geographers have also made significant contributions: Charles Travis, for example, regularly produces new work on literary geography and GIS. His 2020 article for the *International Journal of Humanities and Arts Computing,* 'Historical and imagined GIS borderlandscapes of the American West: Larry McMurtry's *Lonesome Dove* Tetralogy and LA Noirscapes' is just one example. In this article Travis uses GIS methods to bring together 'empirical cartography', dealing with 'latitude, longitude and space' and an 'impressionistic topography' dealing with 'literary, historical and cultural perceptions and experiences of place'. He argues that by 'engaging the concept of Euclidian space with the phenomenology of place, geographers can contextualize field work, and other methods with literary, cartographical and GIS analysis' to generate new approaches to 'the dynamic and symbiotic formations of historical landscapes, identities, senses of place and location' (134). Meanwhile, Anouk Lang has been developing new approaches to literary geography by applying GIS techniques to the study of global modernisms. In her 'Spatial dialectics: pursuing geospatial imaginaries with word embedding models and mapping' (2019) Lang investigates spatial imaginaries 'within a corpus that combines both georeferenceable and non-georeferenceable entities', thereby engaging with the possibilities of working with 'technologies that often mandate binary distinctions and discrete categories to represent and interrogate a world of non-binary human experiences'. Concentrating her analysis on *The Western Home Monthly* (1901–32), a Canadian household magazine, Lang explores ways in which 'different modes of computational analysis might be used in combination to understand how *The Western Home Monthly* was representing place to its readers' (online).

STORY TELLING, VERNACULAR MAPPING, INTERDISCIPLINARITY

Sébastian Caquard provided two progress reports, in 2013 and 2014, which continued the emphasis on online cartography while taking up the topic of 'maps as storytelling devices' and their relationship to narratives and metanarratives. Caquard contrasted story maps, which narrate personal experience, and the 'disembodied, scientific abstractions' of grid maps. He argues that online mapping technologies accessible to the general public facilitate story maps 'by enabling annotations and interactions and thus enabling new stories to be told about places' (Kitchin, 2014: 6). The same technology permits the interface to work more conventionally in the other direction, enabling the places and routes of existing stories and letters to be mapped and shared.

Bringing to mind Margaret Wicke's question of 'how to map space as it is experienced', story maps, or visual storytelling devices, are web-based narratives which combine maps and multimedia content and are particularly important in relation to popular (non-specialist) geographies and the dissemination of geographical knowledge.

In his second report, Caquard turned his attention to the ways in which collective and collaborative mapping can facilitate indigenous cartographies and also the real-time mapping of crises. Part of his point was that these new forms of public mapping challenge the traditional top-down cartographic control of states and corporations and empower alternative forms of individual and collective mappings, sometimes referred to as 'counter-mapping', particularly in relation to indigenous cartographies. Neogeography, another relatively new term, refers to a line of work which looks at non-professional, public forms of geographical knowledge creation and use, typically employing web technology in order to create large open access data sets via crowd-sourcing and freely available GPS/GIS software (Mitchell, 2017).

Kitchin concludes his overview with two publications also from the 2014 volume of *Progress:* Joe Gerlach's article on vernacular mapping practices ('non-statist, extra-institutional, participatory') and Rossetto's argument for the creation of a dialogue between cartography and literary criticism (Kitchin, 2014: 6). Setting out to 'engage with literary criticism and literary texts as sources of unexpected ideas, destabilizing suggestions, and epiphanies' for work in cartography, Rossetto takes the various and different ways in which map terminologies are used in literary studies and cartography in a positive spirit. As part of her analysis of the potential of such a collaboration, she includes a brief case study of the significance of maps and map-reading in Cormac McCarthy's *The Road*, arguing that 'the literary treatment of everyday banal mapping practices' provides literary cartographers with evidence of maps and map readers in action, thereby throwing useful light on the post-representational view of mapping (525). Rossetto is referring here to the view of maps as processes rather than representations, 'contingent, relational, embodied, fluid entities that are performed and manipulated by users in their meanings, as well as in their concrete material consistency' (514). The value of literary texts for this 'processual' view of cartography is that literary 'repertoires' offer 'an immense archive of living maps and emergent mapping practices', and as such 'should be considered as sources, alongside other cartographic narratives coming from ethnographic fieldwork' (525).

The following year, 2015, Rossetto expanded her discussion of map-related terminologies as variously used across the disciplines, concentrating on the term 'post-representational cartography' in order to explain in detail the range of quite different understandings and their use. Rossetto's aim is to sort out these 'different, similar or distant conceptions' and to connect them with 'the broader, well-established debate on the "post-/more-than-/non-representational" within cultural geography' (151). Meanwhile, the ongoing debate over the relative benefits and drawbacks of small-scale studies and close critical reading versus large-scale studies relying on distant reading techniques in contemporary cartographical and literary geography was the subject of the 2018 'Thinking Space' essay for *Literary Geographies* 'Mapping digitally, mapping deep: exploring digital literary geographies', contributed by a group of co-authors connected to the Lancaster University research hub. In order to illustrate the gap between the two positions, the authors cite two contrasting opinions: on the one hand, that 'computational analysis can thrive only in an ecosystem of close reading' (Hammond et al., 2016: 50, quoted in Taylor et al., 2018); and, on the other, that scholars should 'reject close reading in favour of macroanalytic techniques' (Taylor et al., 2018: 11). In their 'Thinking Space' essay the authors argue that both approaches are valuable and needed: a 'full appreciation and understanding of texts, places and spaces depends upon an ongoing interplay between generalization and detailed inquiry'. Their conclusion is that 'the generalisations enabled by advances in "macroanalysis" should not be separated from but rather integrated with attentiveness to detail in both the landscape and the literary text'. They describe how recent work has started 'to combine a distant gaze with close readings to offer new ways of understanding place and space in written works' (Taylor et al., 2018: 11).

TERMINOLOGY REVISITED

Discussing the difficulties of interdisciplinary work even across the various specialisations of geography, L.J. Bracken and E.A. Oughton suggest that 'academics, articulate by nature, are unlikely to question the meaning of a word with which they are already familiar', a situation which exacerbates the likelihood of terminological miscommunication (2006: 376). But as this brief review of work on maps and mapping in human and literary geography has shown, geographers do in fact persistently question the meaning of map terminology, by defamiliarising terms and concepts and rethinking questions as basic as 'What is a map?' So, to recast the point made at the start of this chapter about terminology inhibiting communication between literary geographers and scholars working in thematically related fields: the problem is not so much that terms are used *differently* in literary studies and in literary geography as that metaphorical uses of map terminology typically depend on unchanging and uncomplicated definitions of terms such as 'map' and 'cartography', while literal uses in specialist fields such as human geography and cartography work through phases of redefinition and debate, making those terms unstable and in process.

Tania Rossetto's 2014 suggestion, that the metaphorical use of map terminology in literary criticism might suggest new ways forward for cartographical theory, raises the possibility that the reverse might also be true: that it might be productive for literary studies to take an interest in cartographic theory, as well as the question of how literal maps and mappings work in practice. What, for example, might happen if the idea that authors and texts 'map' narratives was mediated through the kind of nuanced understanding of mapping processes developed within human geography and related fields? Could a 'post-representational' (or 'more-than-representational') way of thinking about mapping stimulate new ways of envisioning the narrative 'mapping' of space in similarly interactive, process-oriented ways? Can the discipline-dependent understandings of 'cognitive mapping' be productively reconciled? These and other possibilities for increased collaboration and mutual support between literary geography and adjacent fields also interested in texts, geographies and spatiality might perhaps be constructively explored.

5

REPRESENTATION

Given that the word 'geography' derives from a combination of the Greek terms 'geo' (earth) and 'graphia' (writing), it is not surprising that representation has always been an important consideration for geographers. In his presidential address to the Institute of British Geographers in 1962 H.C. Darby placed description at the centre of British geography:

> There have been many definitions of geography as an academic study, and there is a variety of opinion about its content and method. Yet everyone – or almost everyone – must agree that, amongst other things, geography is concerned with the description of the earth. The term itself, means 'writing about the earth', by which the Greeks understood 'describing the earth'. Whatever else a geographer may do, the simple aim of describing the earth must appear to him as both logical and sensible.
>
> (Darby, 1962: 1)

Although the term 'literary geography' is most often understood within human geography today to refer to work involving literary text, geographers have also always turned to literary writings as models of effective writing. In the early years, geographers were particularly interested in the writing of accurate and engaging descriptions in clear and accessible prose. Geographers calling for a more 'literary style' in this era were thinking of the 'literary' in terms of realist fiction and the regional novel. This interest in a mode of writing for geography that was literary in style survived in a minor key throughout the mid-century years of positivist and statistical geography, beginning its resurgence in the humanistic phase and making a strong reappearance in recent years with the 'creative (re)turn' in human geography. Where the regional novel and regional geography shared a conventional literary style characterised by readability, the emerging modes of 'literary' writing in geography today are more experimental and creative, with various forms of fiction and poetry becoming increasingly accepted both as research methods and as modes of academic writing.

Alongside this interest in literary representations as models for geographical writing, work in literary geography in its earlier years concentrated on representations of facts, experience and ideology: regional geographers looked to literary representations for objective information; humanistic geographers were interested in representations of located experience; and radical geographers discussed how literary texts represented ideological superstructures (Brosseau, 2017).

> Today, the factual or documentary value of literature continues to enrich geography's pedagogical or historical endeavors ... the humanistic search for vivid experiences of place now examines novels dealing with migration or exile ... and the fragmentation of ideological discourse along a growing number of identity-defining factors (not only class but gender, ethnicity, sexuality and their complex intersections) has reoriented the radical impulse towards the politics of difference and identity in literary representation.
>
> (Brosseau, 2017: 10)

Over time, new themes were gradually added to the original thematic trio of facts, experience and ideology. A growing awareness that both academic and popular geographies generate geographies even as they describe them meant that representation took on additional significance as a theme for literary geographers. As a practice that creates as well as reflects the world, geography actively 'graphs the geo'. The 'new' cultural geography which was developing in UK geography in the 1980s was particularly concerned with the ways in which power operates through representations. Eventually this trend toward the analysis of how representations produce and sustain power relations went beyond questions of which geographies were represented, and how they were represented, to ask who was represented, not only in literary texts and as the subjects of geographical investigation, but also in the literary canon and in the production of geographical knowledge.

More recently, a new approach to representation in literary geography has been prompted by the formation of 'non-representational' and 'more-than-representational' human geographies. Despite the 'non', these approaches do not discount the importance of representation, but instead aim to shift 'the object of analysis from the representation and the system it expresses, to how a representation operates and makes a difference as one part of a relational configuration' (Anderson, 2019: 1122). In literary geography, this reorientation has expanded the focus from 'what a text represents' to 'how relations between text, reader, writer and the world are made and remade through acts of writing and reading' (Anderson, 2019: 1123).

ENGAGING AND INFORMATIVE LITERARY DESCRIPTIONS

One of the original reasons for the establishment of the interdisciplinary field that eventually became known as literary geography was the interest taken by geographers in literary representations of place and region. Ramesh Dhussa and Allen G. Noble have called the era in which geographers turned to literary descriptions for factual information the 'objective use period' (Noble and Dhussa, 1990: 51). One of the earliest works in literary geography, the chapter on 'Geographical novels' in H.R. Mill's *Guide to Geographical Books and Appliances* (1910), emphasises the importance of 'trustworthy' and 'accurate' fiction for geography:

> There are many good works of fiction which are distinctly geographical, beyond the multitude which have 'local colour'. There are some, of course, whose accuracy is not above suspicion; but others are both trustworthy and full in their treatment of scenes, places, and peoples. Assuming that the geography of novels and tales is accurate, a strong case may be made out for their use by students, and more especially by teachers.
>
> (Mill, 1910: 58)

Mill gives as an example of reliable geographical evidence 'the perfect description of a cyclone in the West Indies' in Gertrude Atherton's *The Conqueror* (1902). 'Having once realised the phenomenon by an aid of this kind', Mill argues, 'one can understand and fully appreciate the diagrams and statistics given in books on physical geography' (1910: 59).

Access to reliable descriptions of historical or distant places and geographical events was not, however, the only reason for geographical interest in literary representation: geographers were also keen to take advantage of the lively and engaging style of literary representations. While the 'objective use' period is often described as having been focused on gleaning factual information from literary sources, the literary style of those sources was at the time considered as important as their descriptive content, and literary descriptions were frequently used in the geography classroom to supplement 'more formal and technical studies'. H.C. Darby noted in his presidential address that in the early 1900s A. J. Herbertson, the first Oxford professor of geography, edited a six-volume anthology of such descriptions under the title *Descriptive Geographies from Original Sources*, depicting the world 'in the language of men who have seen it'. Darby also mentions Margaret Anderson's *Splendour of Earth* (1954):

> From travellers, from novelists and others, she collected an array of descriptions in the belief 'that no deadly accurate, purely technical description can bring vividly to life a mountain, a great river, or even a climate, can make it our own to love and remember, as an imaginative description by a great writer can do'. She went on to add that 'we must have the technical descriptions' but that we also needed

'imagery, ideas, beautiful words well used to give full enjoyment and appreciation'.

(Darby, 1962: 3)

In the 1920s and 30s American geographer J.K. Wright also emphasised the value of literary representations of geographical knowledge and experience, believing that some literary authors were 'endowed with a highly developed geographical sense', and had 'trained themselves to visualize even more clearly than the professional geographer [the] regional elements of the earth's surface' (Wright, 1924: 659). Wright argued that while 'a colorless regional monograph falls short of the geographical truth', literary description could 'help make the world really alive to students of geography' (1924: 659). Despite the increasing emphasis on objective statistical analysis in the mid-20th century, Wright's faith in the value of literary representation for geography, and his emphasis on the ability of literary authors not only to visualise place, landscape and region but also to depict them in an engaging manner, persisted in a minor key. Donald Meinig's 'Geography as an art' (1983) and J. Wreford Watson's presidential address to the Institute of British Geographers on 'The soul of geography' (1983) both emphasised the value of literary styles of representation for geographers. Meinig takes Wreford Watson's *Social Geography of the United States* (1979) as an example of the integration of literary and geographical representation, noting that it is 'laced with extensive quotations from novelists and other creative writers on American localities, not as a bit of colour to enliven ... but as primary evidence central to any penetrating geographic interpretation'. Meinig highlights the way in which Wreford Watson's work tried to 'get geographers to recognize that writers not only describe the world, they help shape it. Their very portrayals establish powerful images that affect public attitudes about our landscapes and regions' (Meinig, 1983: 317). Elsewhere, Debora M. Hart and Christopher M. Rogerson remarked in their work on South African literary geographies that a prime motivation for the emergence of literary geography had been a willingness 'to tap the literary artist's heightened gift of perception and communication' (1987: 15).

A 'MORE LITERARY GEOGRAPHY'

The search for supplementary or alternative sources of factual information that were engaging as well as accurate was not the only reason geographers looked to literary descriptions in this era: they were also interested in literary texts as models of good descriptive writing. Efforts to make written geography clear and readable date back to the early 20th century and the work of the American geographer W.M. Davis. Davis was particularly concerned with the establishment of clear terminology, preferring explanatory words which included some reference to origin ('volcano' or 'sea-cliff'), over the simply descriptive ('hill' or 'river'), inventing more than 150 technical terms himself, including 'peneplain' and 'monadnock'. In 1909 Davis read his paper on 'The systematic description of land forms' to a group of British geographers. During the subsequent discussion, Halford Mackinder agreed with Davis 'that one of the chief ends of geography is description' while lamenting that in practice 'good description … is not an outstanding feature of the writing of professional geographers'. Mackinder complained that a word like 'peneplain' 'was not beautiful', and that other, simpler terms such as 'scree' and 'crag' were more likely to 'be accepted readily by the literary writer' (Strahan et al., 1909: 321). Mackinder insisted that geographers 'must seek to use such terms as will fit into literary English writing'. 'I care far more', he added, 'that our terms should be harmonious to the ear and powerful, than I do as to whether they are genetic or analytic' (Strahan et al., 1909: 321). Another concern voiced during discussion was that too great an emphasis on explanatory terminology would mean that geographers would 'lose a certain amount of literary freedom'.

In this era, the sense that geographical writing should be 'more literary' meant that it should be 'better written and more readable', and the literary texts that were understood to provide examples of good writing style tended toward the traditional and descriptive. Aiming for clarity and accessibility, geographers who were looking for models of good descriptive writing turned to the regional novel rather than to more experimental modernist texts. In the 21st century the 'creative turn' in human geography has enabled geographers to become more imaginative and experimental in their writing, but in the early twentieth century this was not how a 'more literary' geography was understood.

A desire to improve geographical styles of written representation continued to result in interventions such as Barry N. Floyd's 'Toward a more literary geography', which appeared in *The Professional Geographer* in 1961. Concerned with 'the role of good writing in the presentation of geography', Floyd cites the 1954 inaugural address made by E.W. Gilbert's as Professor of Geography at Oxford University, in which he had emphasised 'the need for a literary improvement in geographic exposition'. Floyd follows Gilbert in urging geographers first to pay 'stricter attention to English grammar' and 'the sheer structural techniques of scholarly writing', and then to recognise 'the need for that delicate and individual thing which may be called the author's sense of style – his literary sensibility' (Floyd, 1961: 8). 'We are tone-deaf to the use of words', Floyd complained, taking issue with geographers who claimed 'that scientific objectivity and literary skills cannot be mixed' and that 'dependable knowledge should not be confused with literary expressiveness' (10).

This tension between scientific precision and literary freedom in geographical writing, originally noted in 1909 by Halford Mackinder (in Strahan et al., 1909), was exacerbated in the 20th century by the rise of a more quantitative and supposedly objective geography and a subsequent turning away from the literary style. In 'The nature of geography', published in 1939 by the Association for American Geographers, Richard Hartshorne argued that the 'subjective impression' which the literary author 'receives from a landscape or region, and which he desires to convey to others, is something very different from the objective description which the geographer must attempt to provide' (309). Hartshorne argued that the geographical method demanded that 'distinctive personal reactions of the observer [be] reduced to a minimum' (309). Hartshorne believed that 'however effective may be the descriptions of artistic writers in presenting the character of an area, these descriptions cannot be expected to satisfy scientific standards of knowledge' (309). Believing quantifiable objectivity to be the goal of geographical representation, Hartshorne argued that only 'only trained geographers can provide an objective, quantitatively measured, scientifically interpretative, and dependable presentation of an area' (309).

E.W. Gilbert, like Floyd, took a very different position on subjectivity and representation. In his Herbertson Memorial Lecture 'The idea of the region', delivered at the annual conference of the Institute of British Geographers in January 1960, Gilbert argued that 'English regional novelists display many merits that geographers recognize and envy … . Reality is faithfully shown: it is not lost in the dim twilight of modern geographical jargon' (167). The key point to literary representation, for Gilbert, was its ability to produce a synthesis, '"a living picture of the unity of place and people" [Morgan, 1939], something which so often eludes geographical writing' (168). Speaking to the conference at a time now remembered primarily for its emphasis on positivism and quantitative analysis, Gilbert argued that 'regional description can never be an exact science, in spite of its scientific appearance… . it will achieve greater success by the use of artistic and subject methods' (168). Like J.K. Wright before him, Floyd also emphasised the value of the subjective in geographical scholarship. His rebuttal of Richard Hartshorne's argument sustains J.K. Wright's openness to the subjective, and prefigures many of the concerns, values, and practices that would later emerge in postpositivist cultural geography. Floyd contended that the concepts embedded in Hartshorne's arguments should be challenged. 'What is scientifically objective, dependable knowledge?' he asks. 'Can it ever be achieved in reality? Are there any pure facts untainted by subjective judgment or unwarped by the very act of human perception?' (Floyd, 1961: 10). Floyd maintained that 'literary art is not simply a valuable ally of geography but it is indispensable to its highest achievements' (11).

'THE REAL, THE MODIFIED, AND THE IMAGINARY'

The representation of the region in literary writing was an important topic for the early phase of literary geography, with the fictional geographies of Thomas Hardy's Wessex and of William Faulkner's Yoknapatawpha County being favourite subjects. In his 1948 article on 'The regional geography of Thomas Hardy's Wessex', historical geographer H.C. Darby considers Hardy's work in the context of the rise of the regional novel, which he relates to a general interest in regionalism. Darby argues that while Sir Walter Scott's novels 'are full of local color and feeling for country' it was only with Thomas Hardy that 'the topographical novel can be said to have become the regional novel in England'. Darby emphasises that 'the theme underlying the delineation of their characters is man and his work on the land; and the story unfolds through the medium of the everyday life of a locality' (Darby, 1948: 426). 'One cannot fail to be struck time and again', Darby writes 'by the fidelity of this or that scene' (443).

Because the long tradition of work on Hardy's Wessex stretches from the early 20th century to the present day, it provides a useful measure of shifts in the approach to representation in literary geography. In 1981 Brian P. Birch took a different position from Darby on the factual accuracy of Hardy's representation of region, warning that Darby's interpretation should be viewed with caution, and arguing that the primary function of the Wessex setting had been to provide Hardy with 'a territorial frame to help link together [his] rather local, parochial scenes and characters' (Birch, 1981: 349). Birch argues that 'for the purposes of his writing [Hardy] perceived a county rather different from that which one might have seen described in a topographical text in the middle of the 19th century' (351). Birch believed that 'his choice of settings and time periods were governed more by the needs of his fiction than by a desire to reproduce fragments of reality' (351). Charles Aiken's extensive work on Faulkner's Yoknapatawpha County makes a similar point. In an early article on the way in which Faulkner combined the real with the fictional, Aiken explains that Yoknapatawpha 'is not an actual place but a fictional mutation with certain of its components drawn from a reality that was deliberately altered' (Aiken, 1977: 13). Faulkner 'transmuted Lafayette into Yoknapatawpha by combining the real, the modified, and the imaginary'. Aiken explains four main elements in Faulkner's method: 'names were altered, components were omitted, locations were shifted, and reality was blended with fabrication' (1977: 13).

The distinction between the real and the fictional in literary representations of place was also taken up within literary studies. Donald Heiney's article 'Illiers and Combray: a study in literary geography' (1955) considers in detail Proust's manipulation of real-world geographies and the ways in which he blended fiction with reality in creating the fictional Combray. Heiney was responding to a debate about settings in Proust criticism: while some scholars were determined to identify the real-world places 'behind' the fictional place names, others insisted that 'the world of Combray is an imaginary one', and that 'any attempt to connect it to reality is synthetic and impertinent' (Heiney, 1955: 17). Heiney argued that this disagreement resulted from a failure to distinguish between two kinds of sources: experience/memory and imagination/dream. For Heiney, the issue of representation in literary geography lay at the heart of Proust criticism: careful analysis of Proust's use of different kinds of sources, he believed, 'will lead us to an understanding of Proust's method' (Heiney, 1955: 17).

From early on, most literary geographers were aware that literary representation of apparently real world settings would always be a compromise of geographical fact with literary purpose. Virginia Woolf's 1905 *Times Literary Supplement* review of two works of armchair literary tourism famously drew attention to the need to distinguish fictional representations from real-world geography:

> A writer's country is a territory within his own brain; and we run the risk of disillusionment if we try to turn such phantom cities into tangible bricks and mortar ... . No city indeed is so real as this that we make for ourselves and people to our liking; and to insist that it has any counterpart in the cities of the earth is to rob it of half its charm.
> (Woolf, 1905)

Although Noble and Dhussa included J.N.L. Baker, author of 'The geography of Daniel Defoe' (1931), as one of the 'early objective use' literary geographers, all of whom worked on regional literature, Baker makes it clear that he was aware that Defoe had 'not set out to teach his readers geography', pointing out that

Defoe 'used geography for his own ends, and took nearly as much liberty with it as he did with other matters when the necessities of the story so demanded'. Baker emphasises Defoe's 'great skill in blending fact and fiction [and his] considerable discrimination in selecting the facts' (1931: 257). Literary geography has always had to consider this kind of tension between geographical accuracy and fictional inventiveness, particularly in works with apparently recognisable settings. While readers are sometimes dismayed by what they take to be geographical errors in fictional settings, in the academic context only a very blunt approach to literary geography expects fictional geographies to be precisely accurate representations of the lived world.

WHOSE KNOWLEDGE?

While literary texts have traditionally provided literary geographers with engaging representations of remote or historical places and landscapes, they have also provided access to different or historical modes of experience and points of view: the humanistic geographer Yi-Fu Tuan, for example, turned to literary texts not for their accurate representation of historical or distant places, but as a way to access the 'intricate web of feelings, actions, and interactions of that world' (Tuan, 1978: 200). 'What is it like', he asked, 'to be a gas station attendant in the Chicago of the 1920s?' Writing in the heyday of humanistic geography, in the 1970s, Tuan admits the usefulness of landscape description and descriptive writing, but suggests that for the human geographer the emphasis should not be on 'seeing whether a particular street or river is accurately located' but on representations of the 'intimate pacts between persons and setting' (1978: 202). Tuan's attentiveness to the subjective geographical realities represented in literary texts marks a return to J.K. Wright's earlier interest in what he termed 'geosophy': the geographical experience of ordinary people. As Wright explained in his 1947 presidential address to the Association of American Geographers, geosophy concentrates on 'the study of geographical knowledge from any or all points of view' and 'the nature and expression of geographical knowledge both past and present' (Wright, 1947: 12).

Wright's understanding of the usefulness of literary representation for geographers interested in the multiplicity of geographical experience and knowledge made a significant contribution to human geography, establishing the importance of the study of the subjective, and thereby enabling later work on perception and the significance of all kinds of geographical thinking.

> To a geographic establishment committed to the description and explanation of an objective reality, Wright asserted that examination of subjective knowledge might yield fruitful results. The few contemporaries who had expressed an interest in geographical knowledge conceived of it as a cultural trait, generally relevant only in a cultural elite.
>
> (Handley, 1993: 185)

In opening up this new line of geographical thinking Wright accelerated the establishment of literary geography by making the variety of geographical thought, even within what appeared to be a single culture, a topic for human geography: different people inhabited 'different realms of geographical knowledge' (Handley, 1993: 185). Wright's thinking was out of step with most cultural geographers in the mid-century, who took 'culture' to be representative of an elite: Whittlesey's *The Horizon of Geography* (1945), for example, was interested in 'the sense of space current at or near the most advanced frontier of thought' (Whittlesey, 1945: 2). In contrast, Wright was interested in 'all levels of geographic thinking ... both true and false' of 'all manner of people – not only geographers, but farmers and fishermen, business executives and poets, novelists and painters, Bedouins and Hottentots – and for this reason it necessarily has to do in large degree with subjective conceptions' (Wright, 1947: 12).

Wright's interest in subjective geographies survived the positivist years to resurface in the 1960s in David Lowenthal's influential 'Geography, experience, and imagination', in which, like Wright, he emphasises the significance of 'all geographical thought, scientific and other: how it is acquired, transmitted, altered, and integrated into conceptual systems; and how the horizon of geography varies among individuals and groups'

(Lowenthal, 1961: 241). This interest in multiple variants of geographical knowledge connects to the concept of representation not only as 'description' but also as 'representation' in the sense of inclusion: whose perspectives and life experiences are represented? Starting in the 1970s, interest in the geographic thinking of 'all manner of people' took on new significance as feminist geographers began to challenge 'the belief that the "human" in human geography was inclusive, pointing out the various ways in which women's lives and experiences were not considered or included in geographical research' (Gilmartin, 2017). In *Feminism & Geography* (1993) Gillian Rose argued that 'geography was masculinist because it claimed to be universal while ignoring women's experiences':

> She suggested that masculinism had shaped what kinds of research and knowledge were validated, how research was carried out, and how research findings were presented within geography. This broader approach has been used to highlight other exclusions, for example in relation to issues such as race, sexuality, and disability. Feminist geographers also directed attention to the power relations involved in processes of representation, and instigated a more reflexive, self-consciously subjective approach to knowledge generation and knowledge dissemination.
>
> (Gilmartin, 2017)

More recently, postcolonial literary geographers have argued that because literature 'allows for testing out a range of different plausible possibilities and for voicing a range of different perspectives' it is usefully able to 'question the univocality of geographical knowledge' (Noxolo and Preziuso, 2013: 11). In a 2013 article for the *Annals of the Association of Literary Geographers,* Patricia Noxolo and Preziuso took up literary critic Michael Wood's concept of the 'fictionable world' to demonstrate the ways in which

> the accepted unverifiability of fiction, its perpetual openness to reinterpretation, makes the novel a space in which the reader can explore a range of possible interpretations of the factual. In doing so the

reader is not only able to contrast the fictional with the factual but is also able to open the boundaries of verifiability to contestation. Novelists create the possibility of a 'fictionable world', a world that is 'available for conversion into fiction' (Wood, 2005: 158); that is, open to multiple interpretations from multiple located perspectives. It is toward such a multivocal world that postcolonial geography ultimately pushes.
(Noxolo and Preziuso, 2013: 165)

RETHINKING THE 'GRAPHIA' AND THE 'GEO'

Up until the 1970s, work on representation in literary geography focused primarily on depictions and descriptions of the lived world. But two developments complicated the previously straightforward relationship of the 'geo' to the 'graphia', the earth and its writing. On the one hand, the instability of linguistic forms of representation was exposed by work challenging the idea that they could accurately depict the world. Theorists such as Michel Foucault, Roland Barthes and Jacques Derrida showed that words, texts and discourse were not fixed, accurate and universally shared, but instead contingent, contested and linked to questions of power. Foucault used the term 'discourse' to refer to particular social and political systems of representation which produced historically contingent forms of knowledge and meaning. Literary geographers had to start thinking about the ways in which discourse systems shaped geo-representation. They also had to begin recognising that there was no simple, intuitive link between geo-representations and a pre-existing geo-reality. Focusing on the relationship between the signifier and the signified, Barthes drew attention to the inevitable gap that separated words from the things they were supposed to represent. Finally, Derrida's practice of deconstruction emphasised the way in which words derive meaning from their differential relationship to other words, not from their relationship to any non-linguistic reality they may seem to represent.

In this way, work associated with the 'crisis of representation' undercut the idea that the 'geo' could ever be straightforwardly and objectively depicted. At the same time, the relationship between the world and written representations was being complicated from another direction: it was not only the ability of writing to represent the world that was brought into question, but also the ontological status of the 'geo' itself. So while philosophers and critical theorists were raising doubts about the ability of language to represent geo-phenomena, cultural geographers were experimenting with the idea that the world itself could not be separated from subjective perceptions and understandings. The new cultural geographers were particularly concerned with 'the intersecting symbolic and material violences of representations – their often hidden but always powerful capacity to harm and damage' (Anderson, 2019: 1121). A key text for the new cultural geography, Barnes and Duncan's edited collection *Writing Worlds: Discourse, Text & Metaphor in the Representation of Landscape* regarded geographical representation as an 'utterly problematic' activity. The various chapters explored the idea that landscapes, painting, maps, language, written documents and even social action could all be subjected to a form of textual interpretation.

By emphasising the way in which representation is always an intertextual process rather than simply a reflection of 'the real world', the new cultural geography problematised the idea of accuracy in fictional setting. James Joyce's *Ulysses*, for example, is often cited as an instance of accurate fictional geography because of its detailed representation of Dublin on a single day in 1904. Joyce is famously reported as having said that he had intended 'to give a picture of Dublin so complete that if the city suddenly disappeared from the earth it could be reconstructed out of my book' (Budgen, 1972: 69), despite the fact that at the time of his writing the topography of Dublin was undergoing radical change (Hegglund, 2003). Even apparently accurate works frequently rely on existing representations, such as maps, in their efforts to produce historically accurate representations of place, and Joyce made extensive use of maps of Dublin in creating his 'complete' picture of Dublin. According to Hegglund, those maps 'would have derived from the comprehensive British survey of Ireland taken during the early nineteenth century and thus would have represented Ireland through the spatial perspective of an imperial gaze' (2003:

165). In addition, Hegglund argues that by depending on cartographic representations for his creation of a believable Dublin, Joyce 'necessarily engages a specific cultural and political geography of Anglo-Irish relations' (165). Hegglund's analysis of Joyce's Dublin in this way draws attention to the complexity of fictional representations of historic places.

BEYOND REPRESENTATION

In the 21st century, non-representational theory (NRT) has been a significant development in anglophone human geography. Despite the name, non-representational approaches do not deny the significance of representation: as Paul Simpson has explained, 'the critical target of the "non" is more a form of "representationalism" that reduces the world to, and fixes and frames it within, text or discourse alone, and not at representations in and of themselves' (Simpson, 2017). Non-representational approaches consider representations in terms of 'what they do, as being performative and so playing a part in the ongoing shaping of daily life'. Turning to the question of what representations do, rather than what they stand in for, non- or more-than-representational approaches reorient the object of analysis 'from the representation and the system it expresses, to how a representation operates and makes a difference as one part of a relational configuration' (Anderson, 2019: 1123).

In his review of work on representation for *Progress in Human Geography*, Ben Anderson has connected this shift in human geography toward non- and more-than-representational geography with the development in literary geography of the idea of the 'text-as-it-happens' (Hones, 2008). This work considers the literary text as something which happens 'in the course of intermingled processes of writing, publishing, and reading' and which, as a result, because this intermingling is inevitably spatial, 'can be understood as geographical event, or a series of connected events, which have been unfolding (or continue to unfold) in space and time'. (Hones, 2014: 18) According to Anderson, this emphasis on the text as event 'and the vocabulary of "intermingling", "unfolding" and "collaboration" enables literary geographers to disrupt and undermine an ontological distinction between literary and non-literary spaces' (Anderson, 2017: 1123).

The concept of the text as a spatial event involving author, publishers, readers, other texts, reviewers, critics, places and networks is explored most extensively in the 2014 study 'Literary geographies: narrative space' in *Let The Great World Spin* (Hones, 2014). Angharad Saunders, another literary geographer working in this area, has concentrated on the geographies of authorial literary practice, looking at novels not as objects awaiting interpretation, but as spatial processes of making meaning, for example in her book *Place and the Scene of Literary Practice* (2017). Jon Anderson's *Page and Place: Ongoing Compositions of Plot* (2014) is another work of 'relational' literary geography: Anderson interviews writers while walking through places represented in their fiction, showing along the way how literary plots and locations are mutually constitutive. Focusing on fan networks, David McLaughlin (2016) also takes his literary geography outside, showing how American fans of Doyle's Sherlock Holmes have extended the literary spaces of the stories into the extra-textual world through collective reading practices. Abdul Aijaz (2018) suggests that the idea of the 'text-as-event' could be utilised as a methodological tool for going 'beyond representationalism to perceive the co-constitutive nature of the word and the world', explaining that the text 'does not necessarily re-present a world discursively or conceal a world behind it but creates a world in front of it' (151). Finally James Thurgill has developed the idea of a spatial 'hinge' to describe the process in which actual geographical experience mediates reading, but reading then swings back into the lived world to mediate geographical experience (Thurgill, 2021).

THE 'CREATIVE (RE)TURN'

When Marc Brosseau encouraged literary geographers to appreciate the ways in which literary texts represent particular geographies not only in direct description but also through textual strategies such as composition, syntax and montage, he simultaneously highlighted the ways in which contemporary geographical modes of writing and literary texts differed, thereby indicating the possibility of a second wave of the 'more literary' approach to geographical research and writing. Brosseau employed the close-reading techniques of literary criticism in order to bring into view the ways in which textual strategies generated specific geographies: by focusing on the formal properties of the text in his article on *Manhattan Transfer*, 'the city in textual form', Brosseau showed how Dos Passos achieved a depiction of the city that was 'not only expressed transitively but also embedded in the materiality of the text itself' (Brosseau, 1994: 349). As geographers began to appreciate more fully the ways in which literary texts achieve geographical representation not simply with straightforward description but also through formal techniques of style, rhetoric, sound and rhythm, 'literary writing' took on new potential as a model for written geography.

A decade earlier, in 1983, Donald Meinig had admitted that 'literature remains for us a resource, something we borrow from rather than contribute to, something we use rather than something we create as part of the vocation of geography' (Meinig, 1983: 318). This belief came in part from the fact that geographers who were also creative writers tended to keep their academic and their literary identities separate. James Wreford Watson, for example, a distinguished geographer who served as the first president of the Canadian Association of Geographers, used different author names for his poetry and his geography, winning Canada's top literary award for his book of poems *Of Time and the Lover* (1950) as James Wreford. In their introduction to a 2014 collection of articles on 'writing creatively' in geography, Dydia DeLyser and Harriet Hawkins point out that while 'literary writing has long formed an empirical entry point for geographers, offering, among other things, a powerful riposte to positivistic science, creative-writing practices have themselves … long been enrolled as part of the geographer's craft' (131).

DeLyser and Hawkins further noted that while for most academic geographers, 'writing remains the primary means through which we communicate our work' typically in monographs and journal articles, geography had also started to see more 'creative efforts to engage geographical audiences through practices beyond academic publishing' (2014: 131). Inevitably, these initiatives can 'come into conflict with more dominant forms of writing in academia that tend toward clear and straightforward prose' (Boyd, 2017). DeLyser and Hawkins argue that:

> Poetic inquiry ... embraces subjectivity. It is 'involved knowledge' rather than objective knowledge. Participating in 'involved knowing' is to experience it personally, from within, and in relation to others. To re-present that knowing in poetic form is to give it affective charge. In poetic inquiry, the researcher is engaged in a critical act of resistance to dominant forms of academic discourse whilst still working in effective, interdisciplinary ways between the social sciences and the creative arts.
>
> (DeLyser and Hawkins, 2014: 133)

While Wreford Watson avoided any necessity to engage in such a 'critical act' by keeping his 'geographer' and 'poet' identities distinct, more recently geographers such as Allan Pred, Sarah De Leeuw, Eric Magrane and Tim Cresswell have established themselves as geographer-poets, thereby calling into question the boundaries separating geographic and literary forms of representation. In 2011, the geographer Kafui Attoh published 'The bus hub', a poem and a sound recording, in the critical geography journal *Acme*. Discussing Attoh's work in their article 'Creativity and geography: toward a politicised intervention', Sallie A. Marston and Sarah de Leeuw show how it added 'to growing discussion about new and experimental ways of theorizing urban geographies', while 'his music and sound-poetry, by considering urban geographies in creative new ways, demanded that space once more be made for creative practices within geography's own disciplinary practices' (Marston and de Leeuw, 2013: ix). Along with other geographers producing various genres of fiction, these academic poets communicate their ideas in academic style and also in their creative writing, the two not always being easily distinguishable. The use of fiction and poetry as research methods and venues for the dissemination of ideas and arguments in geography is now relatively unremarkable.

6

FUTURES

The plural futures of literary geography lie in three directions: backwards, sideways and forwards. Moving 'backwards' means rediscovering and recuperating the interdiscipline's historiography in order to reconnect it to work in the field today. Deepening our collective understanding of literary geography's origins and histories will help to reinforce the point that the field is a long-term project with traceable roots and a clear identity. Reclaiming historic work should also help to short-circuit repeated cycles of reinvention. Without a clear sense of historiography, work is too easily cast as starkly new and entirely progressive when it may simply be disconnected from what came before. Moving 'sideways' means taking up the benefits and challenges of engaging with fields which provide context, theory and practical input for literary geography, such as human geography, literary studies, digital humanities, geopoetics, creative place writing or cartography. 'Sideways' also refers to the lateral stretch toward adjacent fields which work on related themes but have different aims and methods: spatial literary studies, for example, geocriticism or critical literary geography. 'Forwards' refers to new directions and initiatives emerging and yet to emerge, some innovations already in progress and others at present unimaginable.

As long ago as 1990, Noble and Dhussa believed literary geography was so 'well established' as a geographical subdiscipline that it might have fulfilled its potential: perhaps, they speculated, it had even 'been exhausted as a source of intellectual inquiry' (1990: 61). In their view, 'initial directions have been pursued and original objectives reached', and the best hope for the future was that a 'kind of marking time is occurring during which materials will be digested and gains in scholarship consolidated until a new spurt of creative energy is released, perhaps by an as yet unrecognized scholar' (61). Thirty years later, literary geography is far too active and dynamic to be thought of as 'marking time', but it is highly likely that there are new surges of creative energy already in development, perhaps again featuring some 'as yet unrecognized scholar'.

BACKWARDS

Outside human geography, literary geography today is often misleadingly represented as an 'emergent' or 'new' field. In fact, as this book has shown, the interdiscipline has a long and complex history, and indeed over the past several decades it has been the subject of multiple article-length reviews and summaries, each with its own specific angle or focus, and none (inevitably) entirely comprehensive. Given the field's deep historiography and current pace of development, the writing of a completely balanced and all-inclusive summary would be an impossible task, not least because it would be outdated before it even made it to publication. Part of this continuing development is the uncovering and recuperation of useful historic contributions to the field, inspiring and securing current practice by integrating lost work and building a historiographical platform for the future.

MAKING CONNECTIONS

One of the ways in which literary geography is strengthening its sense of coherent identity and augmenting its collective impact is by making explicit connections between contemporary research and past publications. This enables work from very different eras to be productively read in juxtaposition. Archibald Geikie's 1898 *Types of Scenery and Their Influence on Literature*, for example, is one of the very earliest English-language geographical studies engaging with literary texts, but despite its age it can be usefully connected to more recent work.

One of the features of Geikie's work which can be pulled into the sphere of contemporary literary geography is his interest in the geology which lies below and shapes the visible landscape. Writing in the 19th century, Geikie believed that an understanding of British geology would 'be found of service in enabling us to recognize more clearly the essential features of a landscape', as the 'fundamental elements of the scenery depend upon the nature and structure of the rocks that come to the surface' while 'the manifold varieties of external form arise from the constant succession of different geological formations' (7). He believed that

> while we recognize the potent influence which the scenery of the country has exerted on the progress of our literature, we can look forward to a fresh extension of this influence as the outcome of geographical investigation. Already the result of this widening of the outlook has made itself felt alike in prose and verse. The terrestrial revolutions of which each hill and dale is a witness; the contrasts presented between the present aspect and past history of every crag and peak; the slow silent sculpturing that has carved out all this marvellous array of mountain-forms – appeal vividly to the imagination, and furnish themes that well deserve poetic treatment. That they will be seized upon by some Wordsworth of the future, I cannot doubt. The bond between landscape and literature will thus be drawn closer than ever.
>
> (Geikie, 1898: 58)

More than a hundred years later, Jos Smith took up the connection of writing and geology in his 2015 article for *Literary Geographies* '"Lithogenesis": towards a (geo)poetics of place'. Smith looks at the work of three authors, Kenneth White, Tim Robinson and Alastair McIntosh, finding in each 'a consistent effort to reimagine the cultural geography of place by turning toward a deeper understanding of the stone beneath their feet' (2015: 62).

Beginning with a phrase taken from Hugh MacDiarmid's 1934 poem 'On a raised beach' – 'All is lithogenesis' – Smith focuses on the relationship between stone and the written word. He shows how MacDiarmid's poem takes 'lithogenesis' from its standard definition (the origin or production of minerals and rocks), toward a wider suite of meanings, all of them 'in one way or another revealing the stones as, to quote Alan Bold, "the embodiment of a creative intensity."' Bringing together place writing and poetry, in the context of literary geography, Smith shows how the human understanding of geology has changed since the time in which Geikie was writing: while stone still represents 'the solid foundation beneath our feet, security and durability', there is also an awareness now that we inhabit 'a planet on the move: magma becomes granite, calcite becomes limestone; islands erode, continents drift' (2015: 77).

RECUPERATING AND INTEGRATING 'LOST' WORK

The discovery and recuperation of earlier work has become increasingly possible since the late 20th century with the arrival of digital publication, online resources and search engines. One genre of previously inaccessible works is the unpublished PhD dissertation. Some potentially useful works for literary geography, suggestively dating from the era just before spatial and geographical themes began to gain traction in literary studies, are now accessible online. Barbara Lee Hussey's 1980 doctoral dissertation in Comparative Literature from Purdue University, for example, might perhaps be productively connected to later work. *From Spatiality to Textuality: The Disappearance of the City in the Modern Novel* traces 'a particular evolution in the form and self-concept of the modern novel' which 'culminates in the city's disappearance as a representational space and in its transformation into text' (Hussey, 1980: iv). Among the novels Hussey discusses in the course of this argument are *Manhattan Transfer* and *Ulysses*, both of which were later discussed in detail by literary geographers (Brosseau, 1995; Travis, 2015). Although Hussey's dissertation was not written as literary geography, a sideways/backwards recuperation would be worth considering.

Geosophy, Literature, and the Figurative Landscape (Hones, 1983) is another 'lost' PhD dissertation, this time clearly in the tradition of literary geography. Framed by reference to the geosophy of J.K. Wright, this study investigated the ways in which texts shared within a reader–writer community imply their geosophical contexts, as well as the ways in which an appreciation of those contexts can illuminate the reading of particular texts. Significantly, for the development of literary geography, the study responded to questions being posed in the 1980s by behavioural geographers with an early formulation of the idea of the 'text as event', suggesting that

> insofar as reading, writing, and thinking can be considered to be historical actions, and insofar as text can be considered as historical event, then the geosophical concepts with which I am concerned can be shown to be intricately involved with decision-making and behaviour.
>
> (Hones, 1983: 14)

Another genre of 'lost' work would include articles originally published in print by small journals. Fortunately, quite a few of these are also now becoming available online via PDF scans of the original print versions. Unfortunately, the reader still has to know what to look for, as these historic articles from unknown journals are unlikely to appear on the first few pages of any list of search engine results. 'Humanistic geography and literary text: problems and possibilities' (Hones, 1992), for example, is a critical overview of literary geography published around the same time that Marc Brosseau's influential 'Geography's literature' (1994) came out in *Progress in Human Geography*. 'Humanistic geography and literary text' was published in the *Keisen Jogakuen College Bulletin*, the faculty research journal of a small Japanese women's university. Not surprisingly, the 1992 article has had no impact on the field at all, except in so far as it provided the author with the opportunity to think through issues and establish a platform for later work. While the Keisen University research journal has now been digitalised and its contents are available online, the literary geography articles published in its pages in the 1990s remain essentially 'lost'.

SIDEWAYS

IDENTITY

Exploring productive connections with related academic fields and projects is useful for literary geography, but in order to think 'sideways' it is important to start from a clear position on what 'literary geography' is and does. This means working laterally from an understanding of the interdiscipline as a coherent and defined body of work, with a traceable historiography which functions as a foundation for innovative theory and practice. In recent decades, the general thematic area of work on spatial and geographical themes and literary texts has expanded dramatically, and it is not always easy to determine how the multiple projects working in this area differ or overlap. Many of the fields thematically adjacent to literary geography have capacious definitions: writing in a book chapter subtitled 'the reassertion of space in literary studies', for example, Robert J. Tally Jr. explains that in his view 'what is broadly referred to as spatial literary studies' would 'cover multiform critical practices that would include almost any approach to the text that focuses attention on space, place, or mapping' (2020: 3). Emphasising the inclusivity of spatial literary studies, Tally includes geocriticism, geopoetics, the spatial humanities and literary geography within those 'critical practices'.

While there is a great deal that literary geographers can learn from thematically related literary studies projects such as geocriticism and spatial literary studies, as an interdisciplinary geography/literary studies combination practised at the meeting point of the social sciences and the humanities, literary geography resists incorporation into literary studies. Literary geography is not a thematically defined field with an unstated but taken for granted disciplinary home; it is an interdiscipline with specific aims and methods defined by a distinctive combination of subject and approach. The long history of literary geography, as well as its current theory and practice, are inextricably connected with human geography as well as literary studies, and when that connection is taken seriously it becomes evident that while literary geographers may work and think to some degree like literary critics, they also work and think like geographers.

COLLABORATION

Collaboration between literary geography and adjacent fields is most likely to work when both sides are clear on how they differ. Engagement and collaboration also require those other fields to be aware that literary geography exists. Around 2011 and 2012, as interest in geo-spatial themes and theories was taking hold in literary studies, two articles appeared in the journal *American Literary History* which suggested the benefits that might accrue from collaboration between American Studies and literary history on the one hand and the 'new' cultural geography on the other. To put this in perspective, the suggestion was being made more than 30 years after cultural geography's interest in working with literature had become collectively identified as 'literary geography', 15 years after Marc Brosseau's 'Geography's literature' appeared in *Progress in Human Geography* and ten years after the edited collection of work in new cultural geography, *Cultural Turns/Geographical Turns*, included a chapter on literary geography. Disciplinary gaps, however, meant that the field was apparently unheard of outside human geography. In 2011, literary studies scholar Laura Dow Walls published 'Literature, geography, and the spaces of interdisciplinarity', a review essay of three recent books in American Studies. Walls concludes with a suggestion:

> What we need, I would submit, is not just an interdisciplinary alliance between geography and literature, but a literary geography of transdisciplinary spaces. That is, the boundary separating the disciplines of literature and geography is itself a geographical question, a problem of form which is simultaneously a problem of history.
>
> (Walls, 2011: 871)

The following year, Sara Luria published 'The art and science of literary geography: practical criticism in "America's Wasteland"' (2012). Explaining that 'geographers and literary historians have been moving closer to each other for some time', Luria calls for 'a more deliberate conversation between the fields of literature and geography' as a 'logical next step' (190). Taking as examples the fields of 'critical regionalism, the New West or post-West studies, and more largely environmental criticism', Luria suggests that

> literary historians who work in these fields can engage geographers' work still more deeply. We can get inspiration from the way their field moves more freely between science and art. We can draw upon the rich geographical vocabulary to describe the land we study as a way to refresh our tired metaphors. We can even collaborate with geographers.
>
> (190)

Walls and Luria both make sensible arguments for greater collaboration between literary scholars and geographers. From the perspective of literary geography, however, it is particularly notable that the interdiscipline which had been steadily working at and across the borders of literary studies and geography for more than a century was not even mentioned. As it moves into its futures, literary geography not only needs to look sideways in order to learn from adjacent disciplines but also needs to generate effective strategies to make its work visible and highlight its potential usefulness and relevance.

FORWARDS

INTERDISCIPLINARITY

While literary geography has always had a higher profile in geography than elsewhere, sideways collaboration is not always a matter of stretching outside the discipline. Perhaps surprisingly, the article cited earlier in this book which discussed the difficulties of interdisciplinary communication (Bracken and Oughton, 2006) was actually talking about communication across disciplinary boundaries *within* geography. The emphasis in this book has been on the interdisciplinarity of literary geography as a coming-together of literature, the lived world, literary studies and human geography. However, one of the promising futures for literary geography now coming into focus has to do with the role literary geographers can play within geography as an internally interdisciplinary field. A short 'Thinking Space' essay published in *Literary Geographies* in 2021 indicates the potential which this kind of collaboration might have in the future. 'Bringing literature and literary geographies into geospatial research teams' was contributed to the journal's position papers section by a team working on a US Natural Resources Conservation Service project developing a geospatial method for mapping and modelling inactive acequias (gravity-fed water irrigation systems) in New Mexico, USA. The three team members, a geohumanities scholar-practitioner, a geographic information scientist, and an applied geographer, asked 'What role might literary geography play when practised in parallel with the geospatial science wings?' Following their experimental engagement with various creative media (film, novel, poetry, song) in the course of their research, the team proposed that 'incorporating literary geographic approaches within geospatial research teams can help deepen, texture, and humanize the place-based and particular contexts' of geospatial research projects (Magrane et al., 2021: 147).

TOPICALITY

Because of its inbuilt interest in relating literary texts to the geographies of lived social and physical environments, literary geography was provided with an important topic by the COVID-19 crisis and its various associated restrictions and lockdowns. Starting in early 2020 the global spread of the virus and its associated risks and restrictions had an unavoidably disruptive impact on work and social life. Academics had to adapt their practices of teaching and research, create alternative work spaces, rethink their collaborative practices, and find new ways to participate in conferences and access libraries. Many suddenly had to adapt to working from home while simultaneously coping with the added responsibilities and difficulties involved in caring for others. The sudden shift in circumstances was challenging but also inevitably thought-provoking: for a literary geographer, drastic changes in mobility and access to social spaces combined with sudden shifts in reading habits and engagements with literary texts provided a variety of new things to think about. Literary geographers managing various forms of isolation turned toward new research on literary texts and their links to mobilities, socio-spatial interactions, inequalities, boundaries, domesticity, work spaces and proximities. *Literary Geographies* was able to provide a venue for the resulting work: first, in June 2020 it published a 'Thinking Space' piece on 'The cube of loneliness: literary geographies in isolation'; then six months later it brought out a special issue which included 26 essays contributed from authors located around the world, from Australasia to Europe, East Asia to the Americas, thereby testifying to the growing international network of scholars working on literary geography as well as the global impact of the pandemic. Themes ranged from isolation, to incarceration and memory, to academic practice, to the reassuring rhythms of walking with children while re-visiting a familiar story. A literary geographer in Australia reflected on the likely impact of pandemics and climate change on literary tourism, acknowledging that 'flying across the world to visit writers' houses seems like a rarified practice that I can no longer justify' (Magner, 2020: 282). A geographer working on the testimony of concentration camp survivors detailed some of the ways in which 'isolation' and 'concentration' are not mutually exclusive (Carter-White, 2020). An essay on bird-watching and comfort reading explained 'how text, author, reader, and landscape intersect to produce an improvised sense of healthfulness and well-being' (Briwa, 2020: 213), while reflections on reading Nathaniel Hawthorne's 'Wakefield' in isolation suggested ways to make sense of a 'world turned strange' (Inoue, 2020: 219).

VISIBILITY

In the course of its long and interesting history, literary geography has developed a stronger sense of identity while also gradually achieving wider recognition. The contemporary phase of literary geography can be dated back to the 1990s, a period in which the growing maturity of the interdiscipline was indicated by several reviews of the field, its status, problems and possibilities. It is nevertheless only in the past decade or so that literary geography has started to be widely recognised as a coherent interdiscipline. One of the major tasks for future literary geography will be a continued insistence on its (longstanding) existence. The establishment of the literary geographies bibliography (2012) and of the journal *Literary Geographies* (2015) has had some success in raising the profile of the interdiscipline, and the establishment of a dedicated book series would be a productive next step.

The point to having a book series specifically for literary geography goes beyond the provision of a venue for work in the field within which literary geographers would be able to create a collective and cumulative body of book-length work. Almost as importantly, a book series would finally enable scholars working in the interdiscipline to publish their work as literary geography. When literary geographer Angharad Saunders published *Place and the Scene of Literary Practice* in 2017 it was a work building on the field's historiography while also demonstrating and enabling its progress: her premise was that the act of writing 'is intimately bound up with the flow and eddy of a writer's being-within-the-world', inextricably part of 'the everyday practices, encounters and networks of social life' (xii). Saunders approached the novels she discussed as spatial processes, an argument framed by theory in literary geography. Nevertheless, the book was published in the book series 'Studies in Historical Geography'. On the back cover the press promoted the book as 'key reading for those working in Human Geography, particularly Cultural and Historical Geography, Literary Studies and Literary History', a configuration in which the interdiscipline of literary geography was once again broken down into component parts and rendered invisible. This is why literary geographers are faced with the double challenge of sustaining practice in their field while also defending and promoting it. The main line of future work for literary geographers will, of course, be to carry on expanding and refining their theory and practice. Inevitably, however, a secondary line of future work will involve persistent reinforcement of the point that the field exists, and is continuing to produce work useful and relevant to a wide range of disciplinary and inter-disciplinary projects across the humanities and the social sciences.

CONCLUSION

As this book has explained, while 'literary geography' is currently defined and practised in various different ways, the literary geography which connects and combines human geography and literary studies is a mixed social science/humanities interdiscipline which started out as a historic subfield of academic geography. In common with several thematically adjacent fields, literary geography is interested in the geographies of literature and the geographies generated in and by literature. However, as an interdiscipline with a strong component of academic geography and spatial theory, it also committed to thinking about literature geographically.

This distinctive *geographical* aspect to literary geography derives from the point that the field engages with two conventionally separate areas of study (literature, geography) and two traditionally unconnected academic fields (literary studies, geography), and as a result, the single word 'geography' carries two different meanings. In everyday conversation, 'geography' typically refers to a concept or a physical entity; in academic conversation, it also refers quite separately to an academic field. This can be quite confusing, so it is important to keep in mind that in the term 'literary geography' both of these meanings are included: the 'geography' which we experience, our lived world ('geography in literature'; 'geographies of literature'), and the 'geography' which is the academic practice of geographers ('thinking about literature geographically'). So, in contemporary literary geography, literary text is not just the product of geographies, or the representation of geographies, but is in itself something spatial and geographical. And this is why literary geography takes as much interest in the geographies of inspiration, creation, production, reception and extension as it does in the geographies represented or invented by the text.

It may be that the best way to appreciate what goes on in the always-evolving academic field of academic geography is to focus on practice: 'geography is what geographers do'. This is clearly a circular and somewhat frustrating explanation, but it can nevertheless help non-geographers grasp that the commonsense definition of 'geography' is very different from the definition of 'geography' as the subject and practice of specialist academics. First, the definition of academic geography as 'what geographers do' helps to emphasise the point that the academic practice of 'geography' is constantly being rethought, revised, renewed and re-theorised. It doesn't stand still. It is not a thing; it is a doing, a collaborative and negotiated project. Second, to be clear, the explanation that 'geography is what geographers do' is not exclusionary: it doesn't imply that someone not formally trained in geography is barred from participation. To make another circular explanation: if you're thinking like a geographer you're doing geography – and that is something you can learn to do by reading geography and working with other geographers.

For literary geographers, 'geography' is part of what they think about, along with texts, and also a large part of what they do. But again, this doesn't mean that you have to be a geographer to do literary geography. You can be a literary critic and do literary geography. Whatever your primary disciplinary position might be – geographer, literary critic, cartographer, poet – in order to participate in interdisciplinary literary geography all you need to do is recognise and pay attention to all four of its essential components. And this means, crucially, that when using terms like 'space' or 'distance', it is important to be aware that while these words are used in everyday conversation as if their meaning is obvious, for geographers they are unstable terms permanently subject to debate and theoretically informed redefinition.

Literary geography happens where the writing and reading of literary texts meets geology, topography, landscapes, distances, scales, locations and places. And it happens where literary studies and human geography productively overlap, when critical reading, literary history and reception studies meet critical thinking about the ways in which we experience, make contact with, and impact the worlds in which we live.

GLOSSARY

ANT (actor network theory) stemmed from Bruno Latour's argument (*We Have Never Been Modern*, originally published 1993) that the distinction separating human from non-human entities and processes (as reflected in the historical human/physical geography split) was unsound. Latour pointed out that human action/agency depend on a wide variety of non-human 'actants' (ranging from the mundane to the exceptional). As a result, he and others rejected the dualistic language of people/environment and society/nature and looked to the ways in which people established human/non-human networks, both durable and temporary. ANT has been influential in 21st century human geography, especially in the UK, but has had little effect on the continuing human/physical division.

anthropocene   an unofficial period of geologic time, used to describe the era during which the significant impact of human activity on the planet's climate and ecosystems became apparent and irreversible.

assemblage   early versions of the assemblage idea proposed two contrasting ideas: one, that the world is made up of separate entities connected at their edges; the other, that the world is a single integrated structure regulated by fixed rules. Human geographers reworked this concept to view the world quite differently, as a constantly changing and always in-process product of interactions that are never fully planned or regulated. In this sense an assemblage in contemporary human geography indicates a bundle of potentials and relationships whose stability is always only temporary. In literary geography, assemblage theory has been used to comment on and expand studies of **relational literary geography**.

cartography   refers to (a) the practice of making **maps** and (b) the study of map theory, and the history of map making and map use. Both the professional production of maps and academic thinking about maps were re-energised towards the end of the 20th century. First, technological advances in the capture, processing, storage, distribution and interactive use of data increased accuracy and accessibility, with cartographic capability now readily accessible by the general public. Second, map theorists returned to questions about the nature of maps and the ways in which they record and generate knowledge. In the 1980s, the work of Brian Harley turned critical attention toward the ways in which maps emerge from and sustain systems of power. Where Harley concentrated on analysing the underlying implications of map representations, more recently cartography theory has moved towards a **post-representational cartography** phase, which focuses less on what and how maps *represent* and more on how maps *happen* as they come into being in the interaction of users and makers.

chronotope Mikhail Bakhtin's concept of the chronotope captures the inseparability of space and time. Bakhtin argued that stories inhabit an integrated space–time in which the temporal (e.g. 1941) and the spatial (London) come together to provide a flexible narrative context for events and characters (the Blitz). The dynamic nature of the chronotope provides a useful challenge to the idea of literary **setting** as a static spatial container for action and character.

close and distant reading close reading involves the careful analysis and interpretation of passages of text based on details of content, style and structure. Distant reading is a data-driven digital method used to analyse or tag large bodies of text with geo-referents. Although distant reading was designed to overcome the small-scale range and the subjectivity of close reading, its objectivity has itself been challenged by critics who have critiqued the gendered computational and rhetorical models underlying the process, also pointing out that distance does not necessarily produce neutrality.

cognitive mapping/ cognitive map

cognitive mapping (Lynch, 1960) refers to the ways in which people understand space and how that thinking generates spatial behaviour: a process 'by which an individual acquires, stores, recalls, and decodes information about the relative locations and attributes of the phenomena in [their] everyday spatial environment' (Downs and Stea, 1973: 7). Studies of cognitive mapping consider how people envision spatial relations not only through personal experience but also through media (e.g. maps and diagrams). 'Cognitive mapping' can also refer to Fredric Jameson's 'aesthetic of *cognitive mapping*' (Jameson, 1984), which he envisioned as a rethinking of 'specialized geographical and cartographical issues in terms of social space', considering, for example, the ways in which we 'cognitively map our individual social relationship to local, national and international class realities'. For Jameson the 'the invention and projection of a global cognitive mapping, on a social as well as a spatial scale' is the task of the 'political form of postmodernism' (40).

creative (re)turn

the move in human geography to include literary and creative writing as research methods and modes of academic writing (see also **geopoetics**). Following earlier interest in literary style in geographic writing, as in the early 20th century when geographers took literary place/landscape descriptions as models for clear and accessible academic writing, this 'creative (re)turn' has enabled the advent of the 'geographer-poet'.

critical cartography critical cartography assumes that maps are not neutral or objective. Critical cartographers have analysed the ways in which maps, even superficially 'objective' computer generated maps, articulate and maintain uneven distributions of power. Work on **post-representational cartography** also considers how the practical use of maps generates identities and spaces.

critical geography refers to geographical work aimed at achieving progressive social change and also to critical engagement with the ways in which geographical knowledge itself is produced. Within literary studies, the term has been used metaphorically, as in Toni Morrison's call (1992) to expand the 'landscape' of American literature: 'I want to draw a map, so to speak, of a critical geography and use that map to open up ... space for discovery, intellectual adventure, and close exploration' (4).

critical GIS see Geographic Information Science
critical literary geography in literary studies, 'critical literary geography' is a mode of literary criticism proposed by Andrew Thacker (2005): the 'process of reading and interpreting literary texts by reference to geographical concepts such as space and place, social space, time-space compression, and spatial history'. (See also **geocriticism** and **spatial literary studies**.) The

'critical' distinguishes this academic approach from 'uncritical' popular literary geographies aimed at the general reader, such as gazetteers. In **human geography**, 'critical literary geography' is more likely to be defined as a subcategory of **critical geography**, a practice characterised by its interest in social justice and self-reflexive academic practice.

cultural geography/ new cultural geography

In the late 1980s a primarily UK-based 'new cultural geography' split away from earlier forms of cultural geography based on the approach originally developed in the 1920s by Carl Sauer at UC Berkeley. Cultural geography in the Berkeley School tradition focuses on the 'cultural landscape' – a distinctive physical area 'fashioned from a natural landscape by a cultural group', with the natural area providing the medium, and the local way of life (i.e. culture) providing the agent. Despite a continuing interest in the idea of landscape, the **new cultural geography** drew as much from cultural studies as it did from earlier forms of human geography, focusing on the way in which the world comprised cultural differences. It also worked on the assumption that the human world could not be separated from its representation, regarding culture as performative and always in process.

cultural turn

(1) the move made in geography toward cultural studies and social theory in the late 20th and early 21st centuries (cf. **spatial turn**); (2) a concurrent renewed engagement with the idea of 'culture' in

human geography which reframed it as unstable and contested.

deep mapping (1) an intensive narrative documentary study of **place**, as in William Least Heat-Moon's *PrairyErth: A Deep Map* (1991) and (2) the use of **GIS** in order to explore the material, textual and imagined geographies which combine to form human understandings of particular locations in time and space.

digital humanities a field positioned at the intersection of computing and the humanities. While much modern research and teaching in the humanities depends on computer networks and the access to information online, work within the digital humanities explicitly utilises digital techniques and methods in humanities research projects, for example to analyse data sets that are beyond the scope of individual researchers, as in work in **distant reading** and some **GIS**-based **literary cartography** projects. Closely connected with other interdisciplinary projects such as the **spatial humanities** and **geohumanities**.

distance a measure of extent of separation, an essential part of understanding spatial organisation, and a key concept in human geography. As the complexity of contemporary communications and travel technologies has diminished the importance of physical distance for geographers, other measures of separation have become more significant. A great circle air-route measuring the flying distance between two points, for example, traces the shortest physical (absolute) distance; the physically *possible* 'on-the-ground' route for a pedestrian across a city would be a relative and probably gendered distance, moderated by such variables as cost, time and relative safety. Emotional involvement typically correlates with shorter cognitive distance, while sociocultural distance can be measured not only in terms of degree of interaction but also sociocultural difference.

ecocriticism an earth-centred approach to literary studies, it connects literary criticism with an ethically and morally motivated 'green' view of human-environment relations (cf. **ecopoetics, geocriticism, geopoetics**).

ecopoetics (1) creative writing of poetry from an ecological angle and/or (2) ecocritical approaches to the critical reading of poetry (cf. **geopoetics, ecocriticism**). There has been a recent expansion from 'nature writing' to critical analysis of ecological themes such as environmental disaster.

environmental humanities an interdisciplinary field focusing on environmental topics and problems from multiple humanities approaches and disciplines (cf. **digital humanities, geohumanities, spatial humanities**). The journal *Environmental Humanities* (since 2012) publishes work that 'draws humanities disciplines into conversation with each other, and with the natural and social sciences, around significant environmental issues'.

feminist geography a subfield of human geography since the 1970s that has focused on (1) the ways in which space is gendered and (2) the inherent gendering of academic geography.

fictionable world	a concept introduced to literary geography by Noxolo and Preziuso (2013) in response to the call from postcolonial geography for a wider range of voices and located perspectives. Noxolo and Preziuso suggest that the unverifiability of the novel enables a 'fictionable world' which allows for multiple interpretations from multiple located perspectives. This makes possible the dispersal of centres of knowledge and the inclusion of a more geographically and culturally dispersed range of voices.

geocriticism	takes two main forms in English literary studies, the first closely associated with Bernhard Westphal's *La Géocritique: Réel, Fiction, Espace* (2007) but circulated in anglophone literary studies in Robert Tally Jr.'s translation (2011). The second, broader form of geocriticism was established by Tally as a development of work he had himself begun in the 1990s, also conceived of as 'geocriticism'. The origins of the two forms are in effect contemporaneous, although the use of the term 'geocriticism' to name Tally's more wide-ranging version was established after the publication of Westphal's monograph. Westphal's geocriticism takes a 'geo-centred' approach, putting place rather than author at the centre, while Tally has explained his approach to geocriticism as providing a way of reading literature that would be attuned to spatial relations, place and mapping (cf. **critical literary geography**).

Geographic information Science (GIS, GISci)	(cf. geographic information **systems**) refers to a subfield of geographic information science which interrogates the social and political implications of GIS, and critiques the typical GIS process of knowledge production, e.g. by pointing out its gendered, technocratic or elitist aspects and its association with surveillance technologies.
Geographic information Systems (GIS, GISys)	(cf. geographic information **science**) computer systems which enable the capturing, storage, and display of data relating to positions on the earth's surface. Geographic information systems often show otherwise invisible connections between locations, thereby revealing spatial patterns and relationships.
geographical imaginary	(cf. **geographical imagination, imaginative geographies, imaginary geographies**) an unquestioned way of understanding and organising the world, usually associated with either an *object* ('the geographical imaginary of the American West') or a *subject* ('the 19th-century British geographical imaginary'). A taken-for-granted world view tends to sustain assumptions about organising concepts such as **scale, metageography**, binaries (e.g. culture/nature) and borders, and is subject to critical examination in **human geography**.
geographical imagination	(cf. **geographical imaginary, imaginative geographies, imaginary geographies**) at its most basic, an attentiveness to place, space, landscape and nature and their significance to human life, which allows for the abstract and creative in human geography. The term was

coined by Hugh Prince (1962) in response to the dominance of spatial science in human geography at that time (see **positivist geography**). It was the theme of the 2011 RGS-IBG conference, at which Stephen Daniels emphasised its attention to 'the condition of both the known world and the horizons of possible worlds' (2011). It has become important for work in feminist and critical geography and to the **creative (re)turn**.

geography   academic geography is often understood in terms of a characteristic subject matter: physical features, human settlements, mapping technologies, and so on. Nevertheless, many contemporary human geographers (and geographically-oriented literary geographers) define academic geography not so much in terms of a specific 'subject' but more as a distinctive way of thinking, or a perspective. In this second sense, academic geography is understood to involve distinctive concepts, theories, aims, and methods which it brings to bear on the spatial dimensions of a wide range of subject matter. From this perspective, literary geography is concerned not only with the geographical subject matter or mode of literary texts but also more broadly with the spatialities of literary texts and the literary world.

geohumanities   one of a group of overlapping and interconnected interdisciplinary fields focusing on space and place which emerged after the **spatial turn** (see also **spatial humanities, environmental humanities, digital humanities**). Work in the geohumanities typically engages with both academic and non-academic audiences and mixes creative (literary/artistic) and scholarly outputs. The academic journal *GeoHumanities* publishes articles 'that span conceptual and methodological debates in geography and the humanities; critical reflections on analog and digital artistic productions; and new scholarly interactions occurring at the intersections of geography and multiple humanities disciplines' (see www.tandfonline.com/toc/rgeo20/current). An alternative articulation of the geohumanities was recognised as a subfield of the **digital humanities** in 2013 with the inclusion of a 'GeoHumanities special interest group' to 'address the spatial, spatial-temporal, and place-related aspect of the digital humanities' within the Alliance of Digital Humanities Organizations.

geopoetics a range of practices situated at the meeting point of academic geography and poetry/poetics. In 'Situating Geopoetics' (2015) Eric Magrane outlines three modes: (1) the making of poems (see **creative (re)turn**) (2) analysis of 'poetic' literary texts, usually applying a combination of literary and geographic theory to critical reading (3) theoretical work aligned with geophilosophy. An alternative mode of geopoetics derives from the International Institute of Geopoetics founded in 1989 by poet Kenneth White.

geosophy a term coined by geographer J.K. Wright in the early 20th century to refer to 'the study of geographical knowledge from any or all points of view' (Wright, 1924).

geoweb a suite of geospatial technologies and information freely available online, enabling anyone with an internet connection to create and share data and content.

human geography one of the two main divisions of academic geography and itself containing a wide range of sub-disciplinary fields including cultural geography, historical geography and social geography. Human geography is characterised not by a unique subject matter but by the way it approaches a wide range of subject matter by reference to fundamental geographical concepts including place, space-time, scale, distance and landscape. It draws on a range of methods both quantitative and qualitative from the social sciences and humanities. After the quantitative era of the 1950s and 60s human geography research branched out widely, a diversification which included the emergence of **humanistic geography** in the 1970s, and then **feminist geography** and the **new cultural geography** in the 1980s. The cultural turn and associated interest in critical social theory enabled the establishment of new lines of work including **critical geography** in the 1990s. With quantitative geography still vibrant, and interest in qualitative methods increasing, contemporary human geography maintains a diverse disciplinary identity.

humanistic geography in the 1970s and 80s, humanistic geography emerged (primarily in North America), as part of a critical reaction to the dominant approaches of the time, particularly positivist/quantitative geographies which worked with aggregated models and failed to account for human diversity, creativity and illogicality. Pushing back against what they saw as the way in which positivist and Marxist geographers concentrated on generic figures such as 'economic man', humanistic geographers set out to position human experience and understanding of the world at the centre of human geography, emphasising agency, subjectivity and human values. Leading humanistic geographers such as Yi-Fu Tuan and Anne Buttimer were among the authors included in the foundational *Humanistic Geography: Prospects and Problems* (Ley and Samuels, 1978). Humanistic geography had an important and sustained impact on cultural, social, feminist and literary geography.

imaginary geographies often confused with **imaginative geographies**. Literary geographer Marc Brosseau defines these as 'geographies of the mind'. He takes as an example Luc Bureau's *Géographie de la Nuit* (1997) which surveys how 'night' has been imagined / invented.

imaginative geographies a term associated with the postcolonial writings of Edward Said, this refers to the construction and representation of cultures, people, landscapes and places perceived as 'other' and the ways in which those representations articulate the desires, fantasies, and fears of the authors while embodying and replicating **power-geometries**. Analysis of imaginative geographies aims to clarify the ways in which they are created and their impact.

landscape historically, 'landscape' has been defined within geography in three main ways: (1) an area of land and the arrangement of things it contains; (2) the social and cultural meaning of such an area/arrangement; (3) a picture or art work depicting that area and its features. Early 20th century geographical approaches to landscape focused on environmental determinism (how natural landscapes shaped human societies) and on the cultural landscape (how human societies moderated the landscape through activities such as farming). Landscape was not a main concern for geography during the era of the quantitative revolution (late 1950s–60s) but subsequent work in behavioural geography considered how people know and evaluate landscapes while **humanistic geography** studied lived experiences, senses of place, and the meanings associated with particular landscapes. The **new cultural geography** reworked the idea of landscape in two main ways: first, while some geographers saw landscapes not as material expressions of culture but as complex constructions imbued with symbolic power and susceptible to decoding, others focused on the materiality of landscapes, accounting for built and managed landscapes as products of social relations and therefore parts of the political economy. Poststructuralist geography has approached landscape as a phenomenon always in the process of emerging, which transpires through practice and encounters and therefore requires a relational understanding.

literary cartography currently used within literary geography and related fields in two main ways. With a geographical orientation, it generally refers to practices which either (a) involve reader-generated mapping of a literary text or texts (often using GIS mapping methods) *or* (b) consider the function of author-generated maps embedded within the text or maps included as part of a text's paratextual apparatus (e.g. a map added as a frontispiece to a novel). Such maps might be author-generated or reader-generated. In its more literary and metaphorical use, 'literary cartography' refers to the ways in which literary texts 'map' space and place.

literary geographies the more expansive form of literary geography, the plural indicating that it is open to a broader spectrum of work, running from a more geographical form at one end, through a strongly interdisciplinary centre (literary geography), to a more literary form at the other. At the more literary end, literary geographies adjoins **spatial literary studies**, whereas at the more geographical end it connects with **cultural geography**.

literary geography now commonly termed an **interdiscipline**, literary geography combines and connects work in human geography and in literary studies. It has a four-part structure: the 'literary' refers to literary texts and also to literary studies, while the 'geography' includes not only geographies of the lived world and spatial concepts, but also human geography as an academic discipline.

literary studies a field engaged in the analysis and interpretation of literary texts. Literary studies combines with human geography in the interdiscipline of literary geography, but as separate disciplines literary studies could be defined as a range of critical approaches to a primary *subject matter* while geography is now more likely to be defined by its *characteristic approach* to any given subject. Often conflated with literary criticism, literary studies is also closely related, particularly at times of cultural conflict or transition, to literary theory. Literary texts can be organised historically (literary history) or, formally, by genre (typically, fiction, poetry, drama and film). The history of the book is an associated interdisciplinary field which studies the production, circulation and reception of texts, especially as material objects, from a historical perspective.

literary tourism a form of cultural tourism in which tourists visit sites associated with authors, literary movements or literary texts. Some of the earliest forms of popular literary geography were guides to sites and regions (e.g. 'Hardy country') for literary tourists, and related travel writings for 'armchair literary tourists'.

literary urban studies   an interdisciplinary field grounded in literary studies but also utilising research in urban history, urban planning and cultural geography, it is concerned with representations of the city and with the 'citiness' of the urban condition.

locative literature/ narrative/reading   online technology which focuses on aspects of literary text tagged to specific geographic locations, allowing users (for example) to move through a locality while simultaneously listening to texts linked with their surroundings. The *textopia* project, for example, combined existing and user-generated texts to support the experience of a shared 'poetically augmented reality' (Løvlie, 2009).

maps/mapping   in human geography maps visualise and depict spatial relations, typically highlighting selected features and collating large amounts of information. Maps enable human movement and knowledge of the world. A paper map is usually a two-dimensional abstract and generalised representation from an aerial point of view using scale reduction, a map projection and a set of symbols. Today maps are more likely to be interactive and viewed on a computer or mobile device. Geographers study the ways in which maps both represent and create space (e.g. propaganda maps). In literary studies, meanwhile, the term 'mapping' is often used metaphorically to give the general meaning of 'providing an overview' of a (not necessarily geographical) subject. In human geography 'mapping' has also sometimes been used similarly, e.g. in Peter Jackson's *Maps of Meaning* (1989) which deals with spatial diversity in culture and politics. 21st-century cartographic theorists have argued that maps should be understood not as static representations but as integrated performative and embodied processes involving both map-makers and map-users. From this perspective maps are unfixed and always 'becoming', brought into being by embodied practices typically aimed at problem-solving (e.g. planning or navigation). In this sense maps can be viewed as inherently unstable and ongoing (ontogenetic and processual), moderated by the combined intentions, knowledge and skills of map-makers and map- users.

metafiction fiction which directly acknowledges and makes use of its own fictionality. In literary geography explored by Ridanpää (e.g. 2018) in considering the imagining of space, the construction of regional identity, and distinctions between fact and fiction.

metageography the naturalised organisation of geographical knowledge into categories, e.g. the division of the world's surface into continents. These categorisations are often associated with **imaginative geographies**.

metaphor a figure of speech which relies on the implicit comparison of two things not otherwise alike, e.g. 'a mountain of work'. For a metaphor to communicate its intended meaning to an audience, the connotations of the vehicle (mountain) have to be sufficiently predictable that they help explain the tenor (amount of work) to the target audience. This means that the use of spatial or geographical metaphors first relies on shared and predictable assumptions about geographical phenomena and subjects but also tends to reinforce and sustain those assumptions. As a result, geographers have argued that spatial metaphors need to be used with care and an understanding of their implications, in order to avoid reproducing outdated or oversimplified understandings of geographical terms and ideas. Geographers have argued that 'spatial metaphors are problematic in so far as they presume that space is not' (Smith and Katz, 1993).

more than representational geography   see NRT.

narratology   a subfield of literary studies which analyses and categorises narrative forms and types of narrator.

neogeography   a non-professional, public form of geographical knowledge creation and use, employing web technology to create large open access data sets, often dependant on crowd-sourcing and open-access GPS/GIS software.

new cultural geography   see cultural geography

non-representational theory (NRT) more of an approach than a 'theory', NRT was introduced into human geography in the early 21st century to counter its preoccupation with perception, representation and reasoning by directing attention toward the unconscious, the tactile (or haptic) and the practical. Associated in its early stages with the work of Nigel Thrift, NRT redirected attention toward (1) the importance of the unconscious or pre-conscious in human thought and action, (2) the significance of emotion in human life, (3) the impact of varied embodiments (e.g. pregnancy) on thought and feeling, and (4) role of habit, performance and improvisation in human practice. The shift from representation to 'presentation' emphasised the ways in which people 'do things' as complex thoughtful, emotional, habitual, spontaneous, reasonable and embodied beings. More recently, the alternative designation **'more-than-representational'** has come into use to indicate an awareness of the usefulness of the NRT approach while simultaneously acknowledging the continuing importance of representation.

place once thought of by human geographers as a bordered area of space with a specific identity which functioned as a jigsaw piece in a mosaic spatial arrangement, place became subject to a radical rethinking after the 1970s. With globalisation emerging as an increasingly important force, geographers had to rework their understanding of place in order to allow for an understanding of places as unique not simply on the basis of what distinguished them *from* other places, but also in terms of the uniqueness of their interconnections *with* other places. While some geographers were arguing that globalisation was creating a world of 'placelessness' (Relph, 1976), others were taking the impact of greater global connectivity differently, arguing that with the insides and outsides of places increasingly difficult to define, images of 'nodes' and 'networks' provided a new and workable way in which to establish a view of place as the localised coming-together of multiple human and non-human histories (Massey, 1994; 2005). In Massey's terms places emerge in space as 'localized knots in wider webs of social practice'.

positivist geography characteristic of mainstream human geography in the 1960s and 70s, a positivist approach assumes that knowledge should be based on observation; that statements about the world can be verified or disproved; that facts and values can be separated; and that an accurate scientific method should eventually enable comprehensive knowledge. In the reaction to positivist approaches which took hold after the 1970s, human geography increasingly incorporated the contrasting idea that facts cannot be separated from the values and thought processes of observers, that reality and representation are mutually co-productive, and that tangible/visible events can be generated by intangible/elusive processes. The assumption that a single unified and value-free scientific method was not only desirable but possible was also strongly challenged by the rising diversity of human geographers and their theory and practice.

post-representational cartography understands maps as ongoing processes rather than representational products. In a review (2014) of 40 years of work on mapping theory and practice in *Progress in Human Geography*, Rob Kitchin locates the beginnings of post-representational cartography in a 2000 paper on tourism map spaces which argued that maps are intertextual, that their meanings emerge in context, and that the process of map use co-creates the map along with space, identities and maps. More recently, theorists have proposed that maps are always *mappings* ('spatial practices enacted to solve relational problems') and emphasised the importance of vernacular/participatory maps. Particularly notable for literary geography has been the work of Tania Rossetto (2014) connecting cartography and literary criticism, also suggesting the value of post-representational cartography in the study of maps in literature.

power-geometry a term introduced by the geographer Doreen Massey in her response to David Harvey's concept of **time-space compression**. Massey argued that the idea of time-space compression failed to recognise the uneven power relations which afford agency differently to individuals and communities even within a single location. As the idea of a *geometry* of power relations was not intended to suggest a fixed configuration of power relations, Massey was careful to emphasise its volatility and openness to reconfiguration.

qualitative data a term in human geography which refers to non-numeric information sources, including literary texts, films, music, etc. Although these sources are sometimes transformed into quantitative data (e.g. in **distant reading** and some forms of **literary cartography**) an understanding remains that this process involves some diminishment of the original. Qualitative approaches to geographical research had a resurgence in the postpositivist 1970s, with the rise of **humanistic geography** and the amalgamation of various lines of work in human geography with literary sources under the collective title of **literary geography**. The benefits of qualitative data in enabling human-scaled, interpretative and creative research in human geography are now widely accepted.

reader-response theory/criticism work in literary studies which concentrates on the ways in which readers respond to texts. It moves away from analysis of the inherent meaning of a text and toward discussion of how meaning is produced in the reading process. (See also **text as spatial event, relational literary geography.**)

region commonly imagined as a subnational area (New England) or a cluster of adjacent countries (the Caribbean) but the subject of debate in contemporary human geography. Questions include: (1) Are regions real entities or mental constructs? (2) Are they naturally or socially defined? (3) Are they internally coherent and bordered, or are they disorderly and leaky? Contemporary human geographers tend toward the 'socially constructed' view, also generally agreeing that the identification of clear regional boundaries is problematic. A possible solution treats regions as assemblages characterised by internal variety and permeable boundaries. The region has been an important concept for literary geography since its 19th-century origins, with recent work emphasising the ways in which literary texts contribute to their social construction (Ridanpää, 2017).

relational literary geography a line of work in literary geography based on the geographical concept of relational space. Relational literary geography moves away from thinking of literary texts as bordered containers of universal meaning existing separately from authors, editors and readers, and toward understanding and analysing texts as unstable and always 'happening' in the context of a multi-actant network (see **ANT**). In this sense literary texts can be understood not only as the products of geographies, nor as simply representations of geographies, but as geographical events in themselves. (See also the **text as event** and **assemblage**.)

scale a central but problematic concept in human geography: until relatively recently work concentrated on two main forms: analytical scale and hierarchical scale. Analytical scale depends on precise measurements and is closely associated with map-making and scaling. Hierarchical scales are less precisely measured and thought of as nested categories, for example as an expanding scale from the body to the home, the street and the neighbourhood, through the region and nation, to the continent and the world. Recent thinking in geography, however, has taken the line that, far from being natural or obvious, scales are socially constructed, and there is always an interaction between scales (e.g. the national) and social/political process, which results in a scalar politics. Despite being a central concept for geographers, scale remains hard to pin down: when working from home online, for example, at what scale can that work be located? Some geographers have responded to this problem by experimenting with 'flat scale' where extension is more important than hierarchy ('long' or 'short' extensions) or even attempting a 'human geography without scale'.

sense of place

can be understood as the unique atmospheric quality inherent in a particular location, or alternatively as the perception of such a located quality by the viewer. The concept of the 'sense of place' has also been influenced in recent years by Doreen Massey's description of 'a global sense of place', which articulates place as something 'open and internally multiple' (2005: 141). In Massey's argument, the 'global sense of place' indicates place as a coming-together that is constantly in process, unique but without a clearly separated inside and outside.

sensory geographies	a line of work within human geography which challenges the dominance of the visual by shifting the emphasis to haptic, auditory (sonic/aural), olfactory and gustatory geographies. In *Sensuous Geographies: Body, Sense and Place* (1994) Paul Rodaway set out 'to offer a more integrated view of the role of the senses in geographical understanding: the senses both as a relationship to the world and the senses as in themselves a kind of structuring of space and defining of place' (4).
setting	traditionally considered one of the basic elements of literary text (together with plot, character, theme and style) 'setting' usually refers to the places in which a narrative or lyric is 'set', i.e. located. Understood as 'backdrop', it is a reductive concept separating setting from action and implying a static geography based on the idea of **space** as a 'container'. Understood as a **chronotope**, it refers to a particular **time-space** combination. Arguing that conventional views of setting ignore the ways in which the fictional and the real are tangled together and co-productive, literary geographers have challenged several assumptions underlying the standard (static) view of setting, for example (1) that a simple distinction between real and fictional places is possible, (2) that 'real' geography is made up of named places, is internally coherent and totally knowable, and (3) that the 'real' world has an authoritative geography which can be used to validate or ground fictional setting.

sky writing   the process of creating aerial writing by expelling special smoke from a small aircraft in flight.

space   has been defined in two main ways in human geography: (1) as a container, within which matter exists and events take place, and (2) as the spatial organisation of the world, produced by social relations and practices. The first definition was dominant in geography before the 1950s, although the focus was more on measurable spatial processes than space itself. In the 1970s, the concept of cognitive space (see **cognitive mapping**) suggested that although container space was absolute it was not actually understood as such by people as they lived and moved. Rather, people used their own understandings of their surroundings to make decisions about how they lived and moved; in other words, for most people, their subjective understanding of space (e.g. mental maps) was what drove their spatial decisions and behaviour. Relational understandings of space also started to develop in the 1970s, based on the idea that thinking of space as an absolute, fixed container evacuated it of meaning and ignored all of the ways in which space is *produced*. Marxist thinker Henri Lefebvre's argument in *The Production of Space* (1974, English translation 1991) was particularly influential: his contention was that each mode of production (e. g. capitalist) produced a particular *kind* of space. In Lefebvre's thinking each 'produced space' (1) replicates a mode of production, but (2) also makes possible its opposition and disassembling. This view of space as something produced in social habits and relations gradually shifted the consensus definition in human geography from the 'container' view to the 'relational' view: space doesn't *contain* human life, life *produces space*. Transport networks, cities, 'the seaside' – these are not spaces which exist and are then filled with meaning; they are formed and made meaningful by human actions, and then in turn shape and give meaning to social relations. In the 1980s, feminist geographers took the discussion of the concept of space in human geography in a new direction with the argument that the 'container' view of absolute space depended on a masculinist perspective which regarded space as something that could be fully grasped and controlled from an all-encompassing and neutral point of view. Around the same time, there was a shift toward working with the concept not of space, but of **time-space**. In her influential *For Space* (2005), Doreen Massey makes three propositions about space: first, that it is the product of interrelations; second, that it is the dimension of coexistence; and third, that it is always in a state of becoming. Finally, in recent years there has been a shift toward an 'ontogenetic' view of space, directing attention away from the question of what space 'is' and toward the question of how it 'happens'. Presuming that space is not a definable, knowable, pre-existing entity, this view regards space as always in the process of becoming, thinking of 'space as a verb rather than as a noun' (Doel, 2000).

space-time see **time-space**.

spatial form a concept introduced by Joseph Frank in 'Spatial form in modern literature (1945), in which he drew attention to the non-linear structure of literary works, such as James Joyce's *Ulysses*, in which narrative events are not presented in chronological order but rather distributed 'spatially' across the text so that the reader has to reorganise them into their sequential order during or after reading.

spatial humanities (cf. **environmental humanities, digital humanities, geohumanities**) an interdisciplinary field which integrates geospatial technologies with humanities disciplines to study 'the relationship of space to human behavior and social, economic, political, and cultural development'.

spatiality refers to socially produced space as opposed to Newtonian (absolute) container space. While 'container space' can be understood as a static backdrop to social life (or fictional event), 'spatiality' involves the idea that the social and the spatial are mutually productive and inseparable.

spatial literary studies a subfield of literary studies associated with the anglophone version of **geocriticism** in the early 21st century. Work associated with spatial literary studies often lies alongside or overlaps with work at the more literary end of the literary geography interdisciplinary spectrum.

spatial turn a rekindled interest in space and place across the humanities stimulated by spatial theory developed in post-1970s human geography and philosophy. Henri Lefebvre's *The Production of Space* (1991, English translation of the 1974 original) was an important influence, as was work by Yi-Fu Tuan, David Harvey, Edward Soja, Fredric Jameson and others. Some of the ideas introduced from spatial theory were that space is not a fixed given, that place emerges in the 'coming-together' of histories and trajectories, and that geographies are both real and imagined.

story maps also known as **visual narratives**, story maps are web-based narratives which combine maps and multimedia content.

text as a spatial event a concept developed in 21st-century literary geography in order to engage with the ways in which literary text 'happens' spatially through the networked interaction and collective energy of multiple actors (authors, editors, publishers, critics, readers, etc.). The idea of the 'text as a spatial event' ('text as it happens') recast the thinking of geographer Doreen Massey on **place** in the context of literary geography in order to acknowledge the ways in which a text happens in 'the coming together of the previously unrelated' and as a 'constellation of processes' (2005: 141). From this geographical perspective, literary text can be understood not just as the product of geographies or the representation of geographies but as a geographical event in itself (Hones, 2008, 2011). While it has been influential for literary geography practice (particularly relational literary geographies) it also aimed to provide an overarching theoretical framework for literary geography within which multiple ways of reading and working with texts could coexist.

time-space a combined term emphasising that time and space cannot be meaningfully separated because life always takes place in both. The point of thinking of the two together, as inextricable, is to emphasise that attempts to separate them almost inevitably result in the prioritisation of one over the other. Geographers work with various expressions of time-space, including but not limited to four-dimensional time-space (three spatial dimensions plus time).

time-space compression reduction of the relative distance separating places, e.g. by communication or transportation technologies.

time-space convergence the combined result of **time-space compression** and **time-space distanciation**; the sense that life is speeding up and distances are shrinking (see also **power-geometry**).

time-space distanciation the stretching of social systems across space and time, creating an increased connectedness and interdependence of people and places.

topography within the field of geography, topography refers to the study of the earth's surface.

Topography typically identifies the location of a point or feature according to a horizontal coordinate system plus altitude. Historically performed by surveyors, topographical assessments are now routinely performed at a distance via remote sensing.

topology a form of geometry that analyses connectivity and relative location, in geography it refers to the study of spatial nodes and their positions in networks. Subway maps are usually topological (as opposed to topographical) because the primary goal is the mapping of connections rather than locations.

toponymy the study of place names and geographical features has conventionally concentrated on categorisation and etymology (the history of words), but a more recent **critical toponymy** regards the naming of places and geographical features as a contested spatial practice, acknowledging the ways in which toponyms replicate and reinforce socially and historically uneven distributions of power.

BIBLIOGRAPHY

Aijaz, Abdul (2018) 'Worldly texts and geographies of meaning' in *Literary Geographies* 4 (2), 150–155.

Aiken, Charles (1977) 'Faulkner's Yoknapatawpha County: geographical fact into fiction' in *Geographical Review* 67 (1), 1–21.

Aiken, Charles (2009) *William Faulkner and the Southern Landscape*. University of Georgia Press, Athens GA.

Aitken, Stuart and Deborah Dixon (2006) 'Imagining geographies of film' in *Erdkunde* 60 (4), 326–336.

Alexander, Neal (2013) 'The idea of north: Basil Bunting and regional modernism' in Alexander and Moran (eds), 200–220.

Alexander, Neal (2015a) 'On literary geography' in *Literary Geographies* 1 (1), 3–6.

Alexander, Neal (2015b) 'Theologies of the wild: contemporary landscape writing' in *Journal of Modern Literature* 38 (4), 1–19.

Alexander, Neal and David Cooper (eds) (2013) *Poetry & Geography: Space & Place in Post-War Poetry*. Liverpool University Press, Liverpool.

Alexander, Neal and James Moran (eds) (2013) *Regional Modernisms*. Edinburgh University Press, Edinburgh.

American Tropics: Towards a Literary Geography (book series). https://liverpooluniversitypress.co.uk/series/series-12354/.

Anderson, Ben (2019) 'Cultural geography II: the force of representations' in *Progress in Human Geography* 43 (6), 1120–1132.

Anderson, Jon (2014) *Page and Place: Ongoing Compositions of Plot*. Rodopi, Amsterdam.

Anderson, Margaret (1954) *Splendour of Earth: An Anthology of Travel*. George Philip & Son, London.

Attoh, Kafui (2011) 'The bus hub' in *ACME: An International E-Journal for Critical Geographers* 10, 280–285.

Baker, J.N.L. (1931) 'The geography of Daniel Defoe' in *Scottish Geographical Journal* 47 (5), 257–269.

Bakhtin, M.M. (1981) 'Forms of time and of the chronotope in the novel' in C. Emerson and M. Holquist (trans.), M. Holquist (ed.). University of Texas Press, Austin TX.

Balfe, Myles (2004) 'Incredible geographies? Orientalism and genre fantasy' in *Social & Cultural Geography* 5 (1), 75–90.

Barnes, Trevor (2011) 'Nation and region in modern American and European fiction' in *Comparative Literature Studies* 48 (2), 252–254.

Barnes, Trevor J. and James S. Duncan (eds) (1992) *Writing Worlds: Discourse, Text & Metaphor in the Representation of Landscape*. Routledge, London and New York.

Barnett, Clive (1996) '"A choice of nightmares": narration and desire in *Heart of Darkness*' in *Gender, Place and Culture: A Journal of Feminist Geography* 3 (3), 277–292.
Barrell, John (1972) *The Idea of Landscape and the Sense of Place, 1730–1840*. Cambridge University Press, Cambridge, UK.
Barrell, John (1982) 'Geographies of Hardy's Wessex' in *Journal of Historical Geography* 8 (4), 347–361.
Bartholomew, J.G. (1910) *A Literary and Historical Atlas of Europe*. Dent, London.
Bavidge, Jenny (2006) 'Stories in space: the geographies of children's literature' in *Children's Geographies* 4 (3), 319–330.
Berman, Jessica (ed.) (2016) *A Companion to Virginia Woolf*. Wiley Blackwell, London.
Birch, Brian (1981) 'Wessex, Hardy and the nature novelists' in *Transactions of the Institute of British Geographers* 6 (3), 348–358.
Blake, George (1935) *The Shipbuilders*. Faber and Faber, London.
Blunt, Alison (2005) 'Cultural geography: cultural geographies of home' in *Progress in Human Geography* 29 (4), 505–515.
Bollen, Jonathan and Julie Holledge (2011) 'Hidden dramas: cartographic revelations in the world of theatre studies' in *The Cartographic Journal* 48 (4), 226–236.
Boyd, Candice (2017) 'Research poetry and the non-representational' in *ACME: An International Journal for Critical Geographies* 16 (2), 210–223.
Brace, Catherine and Adeline Johns-Putra (2010) 'Recovering inspiration in the spaces of creative writing' in *Transactions of the Institute of British Geographers* 35 (3), 399–413.
Bracken, Louise and Elizabeth Oughton (2006) '"What do you mean?" The importance of language in developing interdisciplinary research' in *Transactions of the Institute of British Geographers* 31 (3), 371–382.
Bradbury, Malcolm (1996) *The Atlas of Literature*. De Agostini Editions, London and New York.
Briwa, Robert (2020) 'Bird watching with the peregrine: towards literary geographies of comfort reading' in *Literary Geographies* 6 (2), 212–218.
Brooker-Gross, Susan (1981) 'Landscape and social values in children's literature: Nancy Drew mysteries' in *Journal of Geography* 80 (2), 59–64.
Brooker, Peter and Andrew Thacker (eds) (2007) *Geographies of Modernism*. Routledge, London and New York.
Brosseau, Marc (1992) *Des romans-géographes: le roman et la connaissance géographique des lieux*. PhD. Université Paris-Sorbonne, France.
Brosseau, Marc (1994) 'Geography's literature' in *Progress in Human Geography* 18 (3), 333–353.
Brosseau, Marc (1995) 'The city in textual form: *Manhattan Transfer*'s New York' in *Cultural Geographies* 2 (1), 89–114.
Brosseau, Marc (2008) 'The traps: Bukowski as interpreter of cornered lives' in *Anglia – Zeitschrift für englische Philologie* 126 (2), 380–396.
Brosseau, Marc (2009) 'Literature' in Kitchin and Thrift (eds), 212–218.

Brosseau, Marc (2017) 'In, of, out, with, and through: new perspectives in literary geography' in Tally (ed.), 9–27.

Brückner, Martin and Hsuan Hsu (2007) *American Literary Geographies: Spatial Practice and Cultural Production, 1500–1900.* University of Delaware Press, Newark DL.

Budgen, Frank (1972) *James Joyce and the Making of Ulysses.* Oxford University Press, Oxford.

Bureau, Luc (1997) *Géographie de la Nuit.* Boréal, Montréal.

Bushell, S. (2012) 'The slipperiness of literary maps: critical cartography and literary cartography' in *Cartographica: The International Journal for Geographic Information and Geovisualization* 47 (3), 149–160.

Bushell, Sally (2020) *Reading and Mapping Fiction: Spatialising the Literary Text.* Cambridge University Press, Cambridge, UK.

Butz, David (2011) 'The bus hub – editor's preface' in *ACME: An International E-Journal for Critical Geographies* 10 (2), 278–279.

Butzer, Karl (ed.) (1978) 'Dimensions of Human Geography: Essays on Some Familiar and Neglected Themes'. Department of Geography, Research Paper no. 186, University of Chicago, Chicago IL.

Carter-White, Richard (2020) 'Concentration, isolation' in *Literary Geographies* 6 (2), 245–249.

Carver, Evan (2018) 'Graffiti writing as urban narrative' in *Literary Geographies* 4 (2), 188–203.

Clark, Michael Tavel and David Wittenberg (eds) (2017) *Scale in Literature and Culture.* Palgrave Macmillan, New York.

Clarke, David (2017) 'New cultural geography' in Richardson et al. (eds) http://onlinelibrary.wiley.com/book/10.1002/9781118786352.

Colebrook, Martyn and Katharine Cox (eds) (2013) *The Transgressive Iain Banks: Essays on a Writer Beyond Borders.* McFarland, Jefferson NC.

Conron, John (1973) *The American Landscape: A Critical Anthology of Prose and Poetry.* Oxford University Press, New York.

Cook, Ian, David Crouch, Simon Naylor and James Ryan (eds) (2000) *Cultural Turns/Geographical Turns: Perspectives on Cultural Geography.* Routledge, London.

Cooper, David (2019) 'Digital re-enchantment: place writing, the smartphone and social media' in *Literary Geographies* 5 (1), 90–107.

Cooper, David (2020) 'Contemporary British place writing: towards a definition' in Edensor et al. (eds), 634–643.

Cooper, David and Neal Alexander (2013) 'Introduction: poetry & geography' in Cooper and Alexander (eds), 1–18.

Cooper, David and Ian Gregory (2011) 'Mapping the English Lake District: a literary GIS' in *Transactions of the Institute of British Geographers* 36 (1), 89–108.

Cooper, David and Gary Priestnall (2011) 'The processual intertextuality of literary cartographies: critical and digital practices' in *The Cartographic Journal* 48 (4), 250–262.

Cooper, David, Christopher Donaldson and Patricia Murrieta-Flores (eds) (2016) 'Introduction: rethinking literary mapping' in *Literary Mapping in the Digital Age*. Routledge, London, 19–40.

Cosgrove, Denis and Stephen Daniels (eds) (1988) *The Iconography of Landscape: Essays on the Symbolic Representation, Design and Use of Past Environments*. Cambridge University Press, Cambridge, UK.

Crang, Mike (2008) 'Placing stories, performing places: spatiality in Joyce and Austen' in *Anglia – Zeitschrift für englische Philologie* 126 (2), 312–329.

Crang, Mike and Nigel Thrift (eds) (2000) *Thinking Space*. Routledge, London.

Daiches, David and John Flower (1979) *Literary Landscapes of the British Isles: A Narrative Atlas*. Paddington Press, London.

Daniels, Stephen (2011) 'Geographical imagination' in *Transactions of the Institute of British Geographers* 36 (2), 182–187.

Darby, H.C. (1948) 'The regional geography of Thomas Hardy's Wessex' in *Geographical Review* 38 (3), 426–443.

Darby, H. C. (1962) 'The problem of geographical description' in *Transactions and Papers (Institute of British Geographers)* 30, 1–14.

Davis, William Morris (1909) 'The systematic description of land forms' in *The Geographical Journal* 34 (3), 300–318.

DeLyser, Dydia. (2005) *Ramona Memories: Tourism and the Shaping of Southern California*. University of Minnesota Press, Minneapolis MN.

DeLyser, Dydia and Harriet Hawkins (2014) 'Introduction: writing creatively–process, practice, and product' in *Cultural Geographies* 21 (1), 131–134.

Dhussa, Ramesh (1976) 'The perception of home and external regions through the writings of Sarat Chandra Chatterjee: a study in literary geography', MA, University of Akron, Akron OH.

Dhussa, Ramesh (1979) 'Commentary on "literary geography"' in *The Deccan Geographer* 17 (3), 729–730.

Dhussa, Ramesh (1981) 'Literary geography: a bibliography' in *Journal of Cultural Geography* 1 (2), 113–117.

Dhussa, Ramesh (2012) 'Geographic images of Old Delhi through literature' in *Facets of Social Geography – International and Indian Perspectives*. Cambridge University Press, New Delhi, India, 588–601.

Dhussa, Ramesh and Ashok Dutt (1981) 'Literary geography and changing aspects of Calcutta' in *New Perspectives in Geography*, 182–189. Thinker's Library, Allahabad, India.

Dhussa, Ramesh and Ashok Dutt (1983) 'Novelist Sarat Chandra's perception of Bengalis in probash (foreign lands): a literary geographic study' in *The National Geographical Journal of India* 29, 188–206.

Dittmer, Jason (2005) 'Captain America's empire: reflections on identity, popular culture, and post-9/11 geopolitics' in *Annals of the Association of American Geographers* 95 (3), 626–643.

Dittmer, Jason (2010) 'Comic book visualities: a methodological manifesto on geography, montage and narration' in *Transactions of the Institute of British Geographers* 35 (2), 222–236.

Doel, Marcus (2000) 'Un-glunking geography: spatial science after Dr Seuss and Gilles Deleuze' in Crang and Thrift, 130–148.

Domosh, Mona (1998) 'Geography and gender: home, again?' in *Progress in Human Geography* 22 (2), 276–282.

Dowd, Frances (1990) 'Geography is children's literature, math, science, art and a whole world of activities' in *Journal of Geography* 89 (2), 68–73.

Downs, Roger M. and David Stea (eds) (1973) 'Theory' in Downs and Stea (eds) *Image and Environment*. Aldine, Chicago IL, 1–7.

Drabble, Margaret and Jorge Lewinski (1979) *A Writer's Britain: Landscape in Literature*. Thames and Hudson, London.

Duncan, James (1995) 'Landscape geography, 1993–94' in *Progress in Human Geography* 19 (3), 414–422.

Dutt, Ashok and Ramesh Dhussa (1976) 'The contrasting image and landscape of Calcutta through literature' in *Proceedings of the Association of American Geographers* 8, 102–106.

Dutt, Ashok and Ramesh Dhussa (1981) 'Novelist Sarat Chandra's perception of his Bengali home region: a literary geographic study' in *GeoJournal* 5 (1) 41–53.

Edensor, Tim, Ares Kalandides and Uma Kothari (eds) (2020) *The Routledge Handbook of Place*. Routledge, London.

Ekman, Stefan (2018) 'Map and text: world-architecture and the case of Miéville's Perdido Street Station' in *Literary Geographies* 4 (1), 66–83.

Elbow, Gary and Tom Martinson (1980) 'Science fiction for geographers: selected works' in *Journal of Geography* 79 (1), 23–27.

Emerson, C. and M. Holquist (trans. and eds) (1981) *The Dialogic Imagination: Four Essays*. University of Texas Press, Austin TX.

Erdmann, Eva (2011) 'Topographical fiction: a world map of international crime fiction' in *The Cartographic Journal* 48 (4), 274–284.

Elden, Stuart (2013) 'The geopolitics of *King Lear*: territory, land, earth' in *Law & Literature* 25 (2), 147–165.

Elden, Stuart (2018) *Shakespearean Territories*. University of Chicago Press, Chicago, IL.

Eshun, Gabriel and Clare Madge (2012) '"Now let me share this with you": exploring poetry as a method for postcolonial geography research' in *Antipode* 44 (4), 1395–1428.

Fall, Juliet (2006) 'Embodied geographies, naturalised boundaries, and uncritical geopolitics in *La Frontière Invisible*' in *Environment and Planning D: Society and Space* 24 (5), 653–669.

Floyd, Barry N. (1961) 'Toward a more literary geography' in *The Professional Geographer* 13 (4), 7–11.

Frank, Joseph (1945) 'Spatial form in modern literature: an essay in two parts' in *The Sewanee Review* 53 (2), 221–240.

Gabellieri, Nicola (2021) 'Place matters: geographical context, place belonging and the production of locality in Mediterranean Noirs' in *GeoJournal*. https://doi.org/10.1007/s10708-021-10470-x.

Geikie, Archibald (1898) *Types of Scenery and Their Influence on Literature*. Macmillan and Co. Ltd., London.
Gibson, Edward (1992) 'Theory in literary geography: the poetry of Charles Mair' in Simpson-Housley and Norcliffe (eds), 48–57.
Gilbert, Edmund W. (1960) 'The idea of the region: Herbertson memorial lecture' in *Geography* 45 (3), 157–175.
Gillies, John (1994) *Shakespeare and the Geography of Difference*. Cambridge University Press, Cambridge, UK.
Gilmartin, Mary (2017) 'Representation' in Richardson et al. (eds) http://onlinelibrary.wiley.com/book/10.1002/9781118786352.
Gregory, Ian and David Cooper (2009) 'Thomas Gray, Samuel Taylor Coleridge and Geographical Information Systems: a literary GIS of two Lake District tours' in *International Journal of Humanities and Arts Computing* 3 (1–2), 61–84.
Greve, Julius and Florian Zappe, eds. (2019) *Spaces and Fictions of the Weird and the Fantastic: Ecologies, Geographies, Oddities*. Springer Nature, Cham, Switzerland.
Haft, Adele (1999) 'The poet and the map: (di)versifying the teaching of geography' in *Cartographic Perspectives* 33, 33–48.
Haft, Adele (2000) 'Poems shaped like maps: (di)versifying the teaching of geography, II' in *Cartographic Perspectives* 36, 66–91.
Hammond, Adam, Julian Brooke and Graeme Hirst (2016) 'Modeling modernist dialogism: close reading with big data' in Ross and O'Sullivan (eds), 49–78.
Handley, Michael (1993) 'John K. Wright and human nature in geography' in *Geographical Review* 83 (2), 183–193.
Harley, John Brian (1988) 'Maps, knowledge, and power' in Cosgrove and Daniels (eds), 277–312.
Harley, John Brian (1989) 'Deconstructing the map' in *Cartographica: The International Journal for Geographic Information and Geovisualization* 26 (2), 1–20.
Hart, Deborah and Christopher Rogerson (1987) 'Literary geography and the informal sector' in *Geography Research Forum* 8, 15–29.
Hartshorne, Richard (1939) 'The nature of geography: a critical survey of current thought in the light of the past' in *Annals of the Association of American Geographers* 29 (3), 173–412.
Hawley, Edith J. Roswell (1918) *Literary Geography: A Bibliography*. Boston Book Co, Boston MA. https://archive.org/stream/bulletinofbiblio10bostuoft/bulletinofbiblio10bostuoft_djvu.txt.
Hegglund, Jon (2003) '"*Ulysses*"and the rhetoric of cartography' in *Twentieth Century Literature* 49 (2), 164–192.
Heiney, Donald (1955) 'Illiers and Combray: a study in literary geography' in *Twentieth Century Literature* 1 (1), 17–26.
Herbertson, Andrew J. (1901–1909) *Descriptive Geographies from Original Sources Series*. A. & C. Black, London.

Holland, Edward (2012) '"To think and imagine and see differently": popular geopolitics, graphic narrative, and Joe Sacco's "Chechen War, Chechen Women"' in *Geopolitics* 17 (1), 105–129.

Holloway, Julian and James Kneale (2000) 'Mikhail Bakhtin: dialogics of space' in Crang and Thrift (eds), 71–88.

Hones, Sheila (1983) *Geosophy, Literature, and the Figurative Landscape*. PhD dissertation, American and New England Studies Program. Boston University, Boston MA.

Hones, Sheila (1992) 'Humanistic geography and literary text: problems and possibilities' in *Keisen Jogakuen College Bulletin* 4, 25–49.

Hones, Sheila (2006) 'Space, setting, and the adventure story: or, *With Perry in Japan*' in *Genre: Forms of Discourse and Culture* 39 (3–4), 39–55.

Hones, Sheila (2008) 'Text as it happens: literary geography' in *Geography Compass* 2 (5), 1301–1317.

Hones, Sheila (2010) 'Literary geography and the short story: setting and narrative style' in *Cultural Geographies* 17 (4), 473–485.

Hones, Sheila (2011) 'Literary geography: setting and narrative space' in *Social & Cultural Geography* 12 (7), 685–699.

Hones, Sheila (2014) *Literary Geographies: Narrative Space in* Let the Great World Spin. Palgrave Macmillan, New York.

Hones, Sheila (2015) 'Amplifying the aural in literary geography' in *Literary Geographies* 1 1, 79–94.

Hones, Sheila (2020) 'The cube of loneliness: literary geographies in isolation' in *Literary Geographies* 6 (1), 11–14.

Horton, Zachary (2019) 'Written on the sky: inscription, scale, and agency in anthropocenic semiotics' in *Literary Geographies* 5 (1), 54–71.

Hussey, Barbara (1980) *From Spatiality to Textuality: The Disappearance of the City in the Modern Novel*. PhD, Comparative Literature. Purdue University, West Lafayette IN.

Inoue, Hiroyuki (2020) 'The world turned strange: rereading Nathaniel Hawthorne's "Wakefield" in self-isolation' in *Literary Geographies* 6 (2), 219–222.

Jackson, Peter (1989) *Maps of Meaning*. Unwin Hyman, London and Boston.

Jameson, Fredric (1984) 'Postmodernism, or the cultural logic of late capitalism' in *New Left Review I*, 146, 53–92.

Jameson, Fredric (1991) *Postmodernism, or, the Cultural Logic of Late Capitalism*. Duke University Press, Durham NC.

Jarvis, Brian (1988) *Postmodern Cartographies The Geographical Imagination in Contemporary American Culture*. Pluto Press, London.

Jay, Leslie (1975) 'The Black Country of Francis Brett Young' in *Transactions of the Institute of British Geographers* 66, 57–72.

Jeans, D.N. (1979) 'Some literary examples of humanistic descriptions of place' in *The Australian Geographer* 14 (4), 207–214.

Jenkins, Jennifer (2011) 'Out of place: geographical fiction(s) in Håkan Nesser's Inspector Van Veeteren series' in *The Cartographic Journal* 48 (4), 285–292.

Johns, Ewart (1960) 'Langstone Rock. An experiment in the art of landscape description' in *Geography* 45 (3), 176–182.

Kadonaga, Lisa (1995) 'Novel landscapes: geographies of a future North America' in *Western Geography* 5 (6), 24–34.

Kadonaga, Lisa (1998) 'Strange countries and secret worlds in Ruth Rendell's crime novels' in *Geographical Review* 88 (3), 413–428.

Keatinge, M.W. (1902) 'Geography as a correlating subject' in *Geography: Journal of the Geographical Association* 1 (4), 145–149.

Keith, Michael and Steve Pile (eds) (1993) *Place and the Politics of Identity*. Routledge, London.

Kerrigan, John (1998) 'The country of the mind: exploring the links between geography and the writer's imagination' in *Times Literary Supplement* 4980, 3–4.

Kitchin, Rob (2014) 'From mathematical to post-representational understandings of cartography: forty years of mapping theory and praxis in *Progress in Human Geography*', *Progress in Human Geography* virtual issue 1–7. https://journals.sagepub.com/doi/abs/10.1177/0309132514562946.

Kitchin, Rob and Martin Dodge (2007) 'Rethinking maps' in *Progress in Human Geography* 31 (3), 331–344.

Kitchin, Rob and James Kneale (2001) 'Science fiction or future fact? Exploring imaginative geographies of the new millennium' in *Progress in Human Geography* 25 (1), 19–35.

Kitchin, Rob and James Kneale (2002) *Lost in Space: Geographies of Science Fiction*. Continuum, London.

Kitchin, Rob and Nigel Thrift (eds) (2009) *International Encyclopedia of Human Geography*. Elsevier, Amsterdam, NL.

Kitton, Frederic George (1905) *The Dickens Country*. A. and C. Black, London.

Kneale, James (2006) 'From beyond: H. P. Lovecraft and the place of horror' in *Cultural Geographies* 13 (1), 106–126.

Kneale, James (2011) 'Plots: space, conspiracy, and contingency in William Gibson's Pattern Recognition and Spook Country' in *Environment and Planning D: Society and Space* 29 (1), 169–186.

Kneale, James (2013) '"I have never been to Nasqueron": a geographer reads Banks' in Colebrook and Cox (eds), 45–62.

Kobayashi, Audrey (1980) 'Landscape and the poetic act: the role of haiku clubs for the Issei' in *Landscape* 24 (1), 42–47.

Kobayashi, Audrey (1992) 'Structured feeling: Japanese Canadian poetry and landscape' in Simpson-Housley and Norcliffe (eds), 243–257.

Kolodny, Annette (1975) *The Lay of the Land: Metaphor as Experience and History in American Life and Letters*. University of North Carolina Press, Chapel Hill NC.

Kong, Lily and Victor Savage (1986) 'The Malay world in colonial fiction' in *Singapore Journal of Tropical Geography* 7 (1), 40–52.

Kong, Lily and Lily Tay (1998) 'Exalting the past: nostalgia and the construction of heritage in children's literature' in *Area* 30 (2), 133–143.

Kriegel, Leonard (1994) 'Geography lessons' in *The Sewanee Review* 102 (4), 604–611.

Kwan, Mei-Po (2002) 'Is GIS for women? Reflections on the critical discourse in the 1990s' in *Gender, Place and Culture: A Journal of Feminist Geography* 9 (3), 271–279.

Lando, Fabio (1996) 'Fact and fiction: geography and literature' in *GeoJournal* 38 (1), 3–18.

Lang, Anouk (2019) 'Spatial dialectics: pursuing geospatial imaginaries with word embedding models and mapping' in *Modernism/Modernity Print Plus*. https://modernismmodernity.org/forums/posts/spatial-dialectics.

Latour, Bruno (1993) *We Have Never Been Modern*. Harvard University Press, Cambridge MA.

Least Heat-Moon, William (1991) *PrairyErth*. Houghton-Mifflin, Boston MA.

Leer, Martin (1985) 'At the edge: geography and the imagination in the work of David Malouf' in *Australian Literary Studies* 12 (1), 3–21.

Leer, Martin (1991) 'Imagined counterpart, outlining a conceptual literary geography of Australia' in *Australian Literary Studies* 15 (2), 1–13.

Lefebvre, Henri (1991) *The Production of Space*. Donald Nicholson-Smith (trans.). Blackwell, Oxford.

Levstik, Linda S. (1985) 'Literary geography and mapping' in *Social Education* 49 (1), 38–43.

Ley, David and Marwyn Samuels (1978) (eds) *Humanistic Geography: Prospects and Problems*. Maaroufa Press, Chicago IL.

Lieberman, Elias (1912) *The American Short Story: A Study of the Influence of Locality in its Development*. The Editor Co., Ridgewood NJ.

Ljungberg, Christina (2013) 'Constructing new "realities": the performative function of maps in contemporary fiction' in Maeder (ed.) (2003), 159–176.

Long, William J. (1899) *English Literature: Its History and Significance for the Life of the English-Speaking World*. Ginn & Co., Cambridge MA.

Lorimer, Hayden (2008) 'Poetry and place: the shape of words' in *Geography* 93 (3), 181.

Løvlie, Anders (2009) 'Textopia: designing a locative literary reader' in *Journal of Location Based Services* 3 (4), 249.

Lowenthal, David (1961) 'Geography, experience, and imagination: towards a geographical epistemology' in *Annals of the Association of American Geographers* 51 (3), 241–260.

Luchetta, Sara (2017) 'Exploring the literary map: an analytical review of online literary mapping projects' in *Geography Compass* 11 (1), e12303.

Luchetta, Sara (2018) 'Mario Rigoni Stern's "Il bosco degli urogalli" as a narrative atlas: reading the short stories collection with a cartographic imagination' in *Semestrale di studi e ricerche di geografia* 30 (1), 63–78.

Luria, Sarah (2012) 'The art and science of literary geography: practical criticism in "America's Wasteland"' in *American Literary History* 24 (1), 189–204.

Lutwack, Leonard (1984) *The Role of Place in Literature*. Syracuse University Press, Syracuse NY.

Lynch, Kevin (1960) *The Image of the City*. MIT Press, Cambridge MA.

Macphail, C.L. (1997) 'Poetry and pass laws: humanistic geography in urban South Africa' in *South African Geographical Journal* 79 (1), 35–42.

Maeder, Beverley (2003) (ed.) *Representing Realities: Essays on American Literature, Art and Culture*. Gunter Narr Verlag, Tübingen.

Magner, Brigid (2020) 'Regret for sites unseen' in *Literary Geographies* 6 (2), 278–283.

Magrane, Eric (2015) 'Situating geopoetics' in *GeoHumanities*, 1 (1), 86–102.

Magrane, Eric, Michaela Buenemann and Jamie Aguirre (2021) 'Bringing literature and literary geographies into geospatial research teams' in *Literary Geographies* 7 (2), 146–151.

Mallory, William and Paul Simpson-Housley (1987) *Geography and Literature: A Meeting of the Disciplines*. Syracuse University Press, Syracuse NY.

Marais, Sue (1995) 'Getting lost in Cape Town: spatial and temporal dislocation in the South African short fiction cycle' in *English in Africa* 22 (2), 29–43.

Marcotte, Edward (1974) 'The space of the novel' in *Partisan Review* 41, 263–272.

Marston, Sallie and Sarah De Leeuw (2013) 'Creativity and geography: toward a politicized intervention' in *Geographical Review* 103 (2), iii–xxvi.

Martin, Jeff Vance and Gretchen Sneegas (2020) 'Critical worldbuilding: toward a geographical engagement with imagined worlds' in *Literary Geographies* 6 (1), introduction and articles 15–76.

Marx, Leo (1964) *The Machine in the Garden: Technology and the Pastoral Ideal in America*. Leo Marx. Oxford University Press, New York.

Massey, Doreen (1991) 'A global sense of place' in *Marxism Today* June, 24–9 re-printed in Massey, Doreen (1994) *Space, Place and Gender*. Polity Press, Cambridge, UK; see also Massey, Doreen (1994) *Space, Place and Gender*. University of Minnesota Press, Minneapolis MN.

Massey, Doreen (2005) *For Space*. Sage, London.

Matless, David (2008) 'A geography of ghosts: the spectral landscapes of Mary Butts' in *Cultural Geographies* 15 (3), 335–357.

Matley, Ian M. (1987) 'Literary geography and the writer's country' in *Scottish Geographical Journal* 103 (3), 122–131.

McCleery, Alison (2004) 'So many Glasgows: from "personality of place" to "positionality in space and time"' in *Scottish Geographical Journal* 120 (1–2), 3–18.

McCleery, Alison and Alistair McCleery (1981) 'Personality of place in the urban regional novel' in *Scottish Geographical Journal* 97 (2), 66–77.

McLaughlin, David (2016) 'The game's afoot: walking as practice in Sherlockian literary geographies' in *Literary Geographies* 2 (2), 144–163.

McManis, Douglas (1978) 'Places for mysteries' in *Geographical Review* 68 (3), 319–334.

Meinig, Donald (1983) 'Geography as an art' in *Transactions of the Institute of British Geographers* 8 (3), 314–328.

Melville, Lewis (1905) *The Thackeray Country*. A. and C. Black, London.

Mill, Hugh Robert (1910) *Guide to Geographical Books and Appliances: The 2d Ed. of Hints to Teachers and Students on the Choice of Geographical Books for Reference and Reading*. George Philip & Son, London.

Mitchell, Peta (2017) 'Literary geography and the digital: the emergence of neogeography' in Tally (ed.), 85–94.

Moore, Gary and Reginald Golledge (eds) (1976) *Environmental Knowing: Theories, Research and Methods*. Dowden, Hutchinson & Ross, Stroudsberg PA.

Moretti, Franco (1998) *Atlas of the European Novel. 1800–1900*, Verso, London. (Paperback 1999.)

Morgan, Frederick W. (1939) 'Three aspects of regional consciousness' in *The Sociological Review* 31 (1), 68–88.

Morrison, Toni (1992) *Playing in the Dark: Whiteness and the Literary Imagination*. Harvard University Press, Cambridge MA.

Muehrcke, Phillip C. and Juliana Muehrcke (1974) 'Maps in literature' in *Geographical Review* 64 (3), 317–338.

Myers, Garth (2002) 'Colonial geography and masculinity in Eric Dutton's *Kenya Mountain*' in *Gender, Place & Culture* 9 (1), 23–38.

Nadler, Josef (1912) *Literaturgeschichte der deutschen Stämme und Landschaften*. Habbel, Regensburg.

Nagel, Siegfried Robert (1907) *Deutscher literaturatlas: Die geographische und politische Verteilung der deutschen Dichtung in ihrer Entwicklung nebst einem Anhang von Lebenskarten den bedeutendsten Dichter auf 15 Haupt-und 30 Nebenkarten*. Kaiserl und königl, Hof-Buchdruckerei.

Noble, Allen and Ramesh Dhussa (1990) 'Image and substance: a review of literary geography' in *Journal of Cultural Geography* 10 (2), 49–65.

Noxolo, Patricia and Marika Preziuso (2013) 'Postcolonial imaginations: approaching a "fictionable" world through the novels of Maryse Condé and Wilson Harris' in *Annals of the Association of American Geographers* 103 (1), 163–179.

Noxolo, Patricia, Parvati Raghuram and Clare Madge (2008) '"Geography is pregnant" and "geography's milk is flowing": metaphors for a postcolonial discipline?' in *Environment and Planning D: Society and Space* 26 (1), 146–168.

Paul, Alec and Paul Simpson-Housley (1980) 'The novelist's image of the North: discussion' in *Transactions of the Institute of British Geographers* 5 (3), 383–387.

Pearce, Margaret Wicke (2008) 'Framing the days: place and narrative in cartography' in *Cartography and Geographic Information Science* 35, 17–32.

Peterle, Giada (2015) 'Teaching cartography with comics: some examples from BeccoGiallo's graphic novel series' in *J-READING Journal of Research and Didactics in Geography* 4 (1), 69–78.

Peterle, Giada (2016) 'Comic book cartographies: a cartocentred reading of *City of Glass*, the graphic novel' in *Cultural Geographies* 24 (1), 43–68.

Peterle, Giada (2021) *Comics as a Research Practice: Drawing Narrative Geographies Beyond the Frame*. Routledge, Abingdon and New York.

Phelps, William Lyon (1899) 'A literary map of England' in William J. Long (1899).

Philips, Deborah (2011) 'Mapping literary Britain: tourist guides to literary landscapes 1951–2007' in *Tourist Studies* 11 (1), 21–35.

Phillips, Richard (2001) 'Politics of reading: decolonizing children's geographies' in *Cultural Geographies* 8 (2), 125–150.
Phillips, Richard and Scott McCracken (2005) 'Editorial' in *New Formations* 57, 7–9.
Pocock, Douglas C.D. (1979) 'The novelist's image of the North' in *Transactions of the Institute of British Geographers* 5 (3), 62–76.
Pocock, Douglas C.D. (1981) *Humanistic Geography and Literature*. Routledge, London.
Pocock, Douglas C.D. (1988) 'Geography and literature' in *Progress in Human Geography* 12 (1), 87–102.
Porteous, J. Douglas (1986) 'Inscape: landscapes of the mind in the Canadian and Mexican novels of Malcolm Lowry' in *Canadian Geographer/Le Géographe canadien* 30 (2), 123–131.
Porteous, J. Douglas (1987) 'Deathscape: Malcolm Lowry's topophobic view of the city' in *Canadian Geographer/Le Géographe canadien* 31 (1), 34–43.
Prince, Hugh (1962) 'The geographical imagination' in *Landscape* 11 (2), 22–25.
Ramsay, Robert L. (1921) *Short Stories of America*. Houghton Mifflin, Boston MA.
Rawling, Eleanor (2008) 'Spotlight on... poetry and place: introduction' in *Geography* 93 (3), 171.
Relph, Edward (1976) *Place and Placelessness*. Pion, London.
Richardson, Douglas, Noel Castree, Michael Goodchild, Audrey Kobayashi, Weidong Liu, Richard Marsdon (eds) (2017) *International Encyclopedia of Geography: People, the Earth, Environment, and Technology* (1st edn). John Wiley & Sons Ltd, Malden, UK. http://onlinelibrary.wiley.com/book/10.1002/9781118786352.
Ridanpää, Juha (2010) 'Metafictive geography' in *Culture, Theory and Critique* 51 (1), 47–63.
Ridanpää, Juha (2010) 'A masculinist northern wilderness and the emancipatory potential of literary irony' in *Gender, Place and Culture* 17 (3), 319–335.
Ridanpää, Juha (2013) 'Geography and literature' in *Oxford Bibliographies*. www.oxfordbibliographies.com/.
Ridanpää, Juha (2017) 'Imaginative regions' in Tally (ed.), 187–194.
Ridanpää, Juha. (2018) 'Fact and fiction: metafictive geography and literary GIS' in *Literary Geographies* 4 (2), 141–145.
Ridanpää, Juha (2019) 'Dark humor, irony, and the collaborative narrativizations of regional belonging' in *GeoHumanities* 5 (1), 69–85.
Robinson, Brian (1977) 'Some fragmented forms of space' in *Annals of the Association of American Geographers* 67 (4), 549–563.
Robinson, Brian (1987) 'The geography of a crossroads: modernism, surrealism and geography' in Mallory and Simpson-Housley (eds), 185–198.
Robinson, Arthur Howard and Barbara Bartz Petchenik (1976) *The Nature of Maps: Essays Toward Understanding Maps and Mapping*. University of Chicago Press, Chicago IL.
Rodaway, Paul (1994) *Sensuous Geographies: Body, Sense and Place*. Routledge, London.

Rosati, Clayton (2017) 'Cultural turn' in Richardson et al. (eds). http://onlinelibrary.wiley.com/book/10.1002/9781118786352.

Rose, Gillian (1993) *Feminism & Geography: The Limits of Geographical Knowledge*. University of Minnesota Press, Minneapolis MN.

Ross, Shawna and James O'Sullivan (eds) (2016) *Reading Modernism With Machines: Digital Humanities and Modernist Literature*. Palgrave Macmillan, London.

Rossetto, Tania (2014) 'Theorizing maps with literature' in *Progress in Human Geography* 38 (4), 513–530.

Rossetto, Tania (2015) 'Semantic ruminations on "post-representational cartography"' in *International Journal of Cartography* 1 (2), 151–167.

Salter, Christopher (1978) 'Signatures and settings: one approach to landscape in literature', in Butzer (ed.), 69–83.

Salter, Christopher L. and William J. Lloyd (1977) 'Landscape in Literature', Association of American Geographers, Washington DC. Resource Papers for College Geography No. 76-3.

Sandberg, L. Anders and John S. Marsh (1988) 'Focus: literary landscapes; geography and literature' in *The Canadian Geographer/Le Géographe canadien*, 32 (3), 266–276.

Sanders, Julie (2011) *The Cultural Geography of Early Modern Drama, 1620–1650*. Cambridge University Press, Cambridge, UK. (Publisher's online summary: www.cambridge.org/core/books/cultural-geography-of-early-modern-drama-16201650/78DD6853B46EB302E6B8A8964DC2F0AC#fndtn-information.)

Sauer, Carl O. (1941) 'Foreword to historical geography' in *Annals of the Association of American Geographers* 31 (1), 1–24.

Sauer, Carl (1963) 'The Morphology of Landscape' in *Land and Life: A Selection of the Writings of Carl Ortwin Sauer*, edited by John Leighly, 315–350. University of California Press, Berkeley CA (original work published in 1925.)

Saunders, Angharad (2010) 'Literary geography: reforging the connections' in *Progress in Human Geography* 34 (4), 1–17.

Saunders, Angharad (2015) 'Interpretations on an interior' in *Literary Geographies* 1 (2), 174–194.

Saunders, Angharad. (2017) *Place and the Scene of Literary Practice*. Routledge, London.

Seamon, D. (1976) 'Phenomenological investigation of imaginative literature: a commentary' in Moore and Golledge (eds), 286–290.

Sharp, Joanne (1994) 'A topology of "post" nationality: (re)mapping identity in the *Satanic Verses*' in *Cultural Geographies* 1 (1), 65–76.

Sharp, Joanne (1996) 'Locating imaginary homelands: literature, geography, and Salman Rushdie' in *GeoJournal* 38 (1), 119–127.

Sharp, Joanne (2000) 'Towards a critical analysis of fictive geographies' in *Area* 32 (3), 327–334.

Sharp, Joanne (2003) 'Feminist and postcolonial engagements' in *A Companion to Political Geography* 7, 59–74.

Sharp, William (1904) *Literary Geography*. Pall Mall Publications, London.

Simpson-Housley, Paul and Glen Norcliffe (eds) (1992) *A Few Acres of Snow: Literary and Artistic Images of Canada*. Dundurn, Toronto ON.

Simpson, Paul (2017) 'Nonrepresentational theory' in Richardson et al. (eds) http://onlinelibrary.wiley.com/book/10.1002/9781118786352.

Smith, Henry Nash (1950) *Virgin Land: The American West as Symbol and Myth*. Harvard University Press, Boston MA.

Smith, Jos (2015) '"Lithogenesis": towards a (geo)poetics of place' in *Literary Geographies* 1 (1), 62–78.

Smith, Neil and Cindi Katz (1993) 'Towards a spatialized politics' in Keith and Pile (eds), 66–81.

Strahan, Aubrey, et al. (1909) 'The systematic description of land forms: discussion' in *Geographical Journal* 34 (3), 318–326.

Strauss, Kendra (2015) 'These overheating worlds' in *Annals of the Association of American Geographers* 105 (2), 342–350.

Stuart, J. Erskine (1888) *The Brontë Country: Its Topography, Antiquities, and History*. Longmans, Green & Co., London.

Stuart, J. Erskine (1892) *The Literary Shrines of Yorkshire*. Longmans, Green & Co., London.

Surgeoner, Joanna (2007) 'A feminist literary cartography of the Canadian north: women, writing and place in Aritha van Herk's *Places Far From Ellesmere*' in *Gender, Place & Culture* 14 (6), 641–658.

Tally Jr., Robert T. (2013) *Spatiality*. Routledge, New York and London.

Tally Jr., Robert T. (2017) 'Introduction: the reassertion of space in literary studies' in Tally (ed.) *The Routledge Handbook of Literature and Space*. Routledge, New York and London, 1–6.

Tally Jr., Robert T. (2020) 'Spatial literary studies' in *Literary Geographies* 6 (1), 1–4.

Taylor, Joanna, Christopher E. Donaldson, Ian N. Gregory and James O. Butler (2018) 'Mapping digitally, mapping deep: exploring digital literary geographies' in *Literary Geographies* 4 (1), 10–19.

Thacker, Andrew (2003) *Moving Through Modernity: Space and Geography in Modernism*. Manchester University Press, Manchester, UK.

Thacker, Andrew (2005) 'The idea of a critical literary geography' in *New Formations* 57, 56–73.

Thacker, Andrew (2016) 'Woolf and geography' in Berman, J. (ed.) *A Companion to Virginia Woolf*. Wiley Blackwell, London, 411–425.

Thurgill, James (2018) 'Extra-textual encounters: locating place in the text-as-event: an experiential reading of M.R. James' "A Warning to the Curious"' in *Literary Geographies* 4 (2), 221–244.

Thurgill, James (2021) 'Literary geography and the spatial hinge' in *Literary Geographies* 7 (2), 152–156.

Tomaney, John (2007) 'Keeping a beat in the dark: narratives of regional identity in Basil Bunting's *Briggflatts*' in *Environment and Planning D: Society and Space* 25 (2), 355–375.

Trachtenberg, Alan (1979) *Brooklyn Bridge: Fact and Symbol*. University of Chicago Press, Chicago IL.

Travis, Charles (2015) 'Visual geo-literary and historical analysis, tweetflickrtubing, and James Joyce's *Ulysses* (1922)' in *Annals of the Association of American Geographers* 105 (5), 927–950.

Travis, Charles (2020) 'Historical and imagined GIS borderlandscapes of the American West: Larry McMurtry's *Lonesome Dove* Tetralogy and LA Noirscapes' in *International Journal of Humanities and Arts Computing* 14 (1–2), 134–153.

Tuan, Yi-Fu (1976) 'Literature, experience and environmental knowing' in Moore and Golledge (eds), 260–272.

Tuan, Yi-Fu (1978) 'Literature and geography: implications for geographical research' in Ley and Samuels (eds), 194–206.

Tuan, Yi-Fu (1985) 'The landscapes of Sherlock Holmes' in *Journal of Geography* 84 (2), 56–60.

Tyner, James, Soksvisal Kimsroy and Savina Sirik (2015) 'Nature, poetry, and public pedagogy: the poetic geographies of the Khmer Rouge' in *Annals of the Association of American Geographers* 105 (6), 1285–1299.

Walls, L.D. (2011) 'Literature, geography, and the spaces of interdisciplinarity' in *American Literary History* 23 (4), 860–872.

Wang, Xiao-lun (1990) 'Geography and Chinese poetry' in *Geographical Review* 80 (1), 43–55.

Watson, J. Wreford (1965) 'Canadian regionalism in life and letters' in *Geographical Journal* 131 (1), 21–33.

Watson, J. Wreford (1979) *Social Geography of the United States*. Longman Publishing Group, Harlow, Essex.

Watson, J. Wreford (1983) 'The soul of geography' in *Transactions of the Institute of British Geographers* 8 (4), 385–399.

Westphal, Bernhard (2007) *La Géocritique: Réel, Fiction, Espace*. Les Éditions des Minuits, Paris.

Westphal, Bernhard (2011) *Geocriticism: Real and Fictional Spaces*. Robert T. Tally, Jr. (trans.). Palgrave Macmillan, New York.

Wharton, D. (ed.) (1920) *Short List of Novels and Literary Works of Geographic Interest*. Leeds Branch of the British Geographers Association, London.

Whittlesey, Derwent (1945) 'The horizon of geography' in *Annals of the Association of American Geographers* 35 (1), 1–36.

Williams, Raymond (1973) *The Country and the City*. Chatto & Windus, London.

Women and Geography Study Group (2014) *Feminist Geographies: Explorations in Diversity and Difference*. Routledge, London.

Women and Geography Study Group of the IBG (1984) *Geography and Gender: An introduction to Feminist Geography*. Hutchinson Educational Ltd in association with the Explorations in Feminism Collective.

Wood, Michael (2005) *Literature and the Taste of Knowledge*. Cambridge University Press, Cambridge, UK.

Woods, Maxwell (2018) 'Imagining the anthropocenic city: the new face of urban renewal in New Orleans and Josh Neufeld's *AD: New Orleans After the Deluge*' in *Literary Geographies* 4 (1), 84–102.

Woolf, Virginia (1905) 'Literary geography' in *Times Literary Supplement*, Friday, March 10 Issue 165, 81.

Wreford, James (1950) *Of Time and the Lover*. McClelland & Stewart, Toronto.

Wright, John Kirtland (unsigned) (1924) 'Geography in literature' in *The Geographical Review* 14 (4), 659–660.

Wright, John Kirtland (1926) 'A plea for the history of geography' in *Isis* 8 (3), 477–491.

Wright, John Kirtland (1947) 'Terrae incognitae: the place of the imagination in geography' in *Annals of the Association of American Geographers* 37 (1), 1–15.

Wylie, John (2000) 'New and old worlds: *The Tempest* and early colonial discourse' in *Social & Cultural Geography* 1 (1), 45–63.

INDEX

Note: **entries in bold** have entries in the glossary, with the page number for the glossary entry also in **bold**

Alexander, Neal 3, 5, 10, 32, 67, 68
American Studies 10, 35–6, 130, 132
anthropocene 83–4, **140**

Bakhtin, M. M. 15, 33, 141
Brosseau, Marc 24–6, 41, 58, 65, 132; and French language literary geography 31; on genre 58; 'Geography's Literature' (1994) 41, 58, 124, 130, 132; on imaginary geographies 152; on literary geographies of modernism 68; on *Manhattan Transfer* 33–4, 124, 129; on the novel as geographer 31, 123–4; overviews of literary geography 41, 58, 108, 124, 130; on the short story 45, 81

cartography Chapter 4 *passim*; critical 74, 89, 94–9, **143**; **post-representational** 89, 92, 96–98, 104–6, 141,143, **160**; processual cartography 76–7, 98, 105, 156; *see also* Geographic Information Systems; Geographic Information Science; literary cartography
children's fiction 39, 64, 75–6, 135
chronotope 15, 33–4, **141**
cities (*see also* urban) 38, 71, 83–4, 88, 124, 129, 155; children's experiences of 76; Indian 38; in modernist fiction 34, 40, 68, 124; in detective fiction 73; and nostalgia 76; real and imagined (Woolf) 116; in *Ulysses* 121; *see also* graffiti
climate change, 'cli-fi' 79, 83, 84, 135, 140

close and distant reading 105, **141**, 161; close critical reading 48, 75, 78, 124; data-driven analysis 6, 105, 145, 161
cognitive mapping/cognitive map 20, 88–9, 106, **142**, 145, 165
comic books 66, 82–3
Cooper, David 68, 72, 76–7, 84–5, 87, 98, 99
creative (re)turn 49, 108, 123–5, **142**, 148, 150
crime fiction 65, 72–5
critical geography 32, 51, 125, **143**, 148, 151
critical GIS *see* Geographic Information Science
critical literary geography, various definitions of 20, 48, 58, **144**; in human geography 48, 51; in literary studies 7–8, 10, 18, 68, 101, 126; and Kerrigan's 'Country of the Mind' 24
cultural geography 71, 118, 121, 132, **144**, 154; and landscape 152–3; 'new' cultural geography 16–17, 109, 121, 132, 151; and **non-representational theory** 105; post-positivist 37, 54, 114; as subfield of human geography 150–1; *see also* creative (re)turn
cultural studies 10, 16–17, 24, 35, 42, 54, **144**
cultural turn 10–11, 16–17, 97, 132, **144**, 151

Darby, H.C. 36, 55–6, 91, 107, 110–11, 115
Dhussa, Ramesh 2, 26–7, 30, 38, 41, 109, 116, 127

detective fiction *see* crime fiction
digital humanities 44, 102, 126, **145**
distance 75–6, 138, 142, **145**, 151; in
 time-space compression 169; in
 time-space distanciation 169
distant reading *see* **close and distant reading**
drama 70–1

ecocriticism 17, **146**
ecopoetics 147
environment 5, 17, 45, 78–9; and cognitive mapping 88; **142;** environmental criticism 133; environmental determinism 28, 54, 152; **environmental humanities 146;** environmental perception 49; *see also* **ecocriticism; ecopoetics**

fantasy fiction 78–80, 83
Faulkner, William 39, 94, 114–5
feminist geography 9, 97, 119, **146**; and concepts of space 166; and critical readings 36, 52, 75, 83; and GIS 97; and humanistic geography 151–2
fictionable world/s 78, 79, 119–20, **146**
Frank, Joseph *see* **spatial form**

Geikie, Archibald 15, 29, 30, 128–29
gender 52, 145, 146, 147; and distant reading 141; and GIS 97, 147; in human geography 9, 51–2; in literary geography 75, 83, 97, 108
geocriticism 7–9, **148**, 167; and literary geography 18, 21, 131; *see also* **spatial literary studies**
geographer-poet 68, 69, 125, 142
Geographic information Science (GIS, GISci) 95, 97, **147**
Geographic information Systems (GIS, GISy) 13, 87, 94–104, **147–8,** 153; and deep mapping 144; and digital humanities 145; and neogeograhy 158
geographical imaginary 52, **148**

geographical imagination 29, 47, 76, **148**
geography, as a component of literary geography 1, 8–9, 137, **150**; writing style in, 29, 49–51, 72, 107–8, 111–14, 123–5
geohumanities 3, 134, 145, **149**
geopoetics 44, 126, 142, 146, **150**
geopolitics 17, 71, 82–3
geosophy 28, 29, 117, 130, **150**
geoweb 91, 94, **150**
ghost stories and tales of the supernatural 80
graffiti 66, 84
graphic fiction 82–4

Hardy, Thomas 36, 40, 45–6, 55–6, 91, 114–15, 155
Harley, J.B. 12, 89, 95–6, 141
Hones, Sheila 60–2, 122–3, 130, 168; and interspatiality 122–3; on setting in the short story 81; on space and adventure fiction 75; on the spatiality of literary geography 60–2; 'text as it happens' 122–3; *see also* **relational literary geography; text as a spatial event**
humanistic geography 24, 54, 69, 117, 130

imaginative geographies 28, 79, **152**
interspatiality *see* 'literary' and 'actual-world' geographies

Jameson, Fredric 88–9, 142, 168

Kerrigan, John, 'The Country of the Mind' 24–9, 32, 36, 40, 42, 55, 57
Kitchin, Rob 77, 79, 90, 92–104, 160
Kneale, James 9, 33, 46, 79

landscape, 73– 84 *passim,* 128, **152;** American 35–6, 111; landscape geography 25; literary 40–1; 'landscape in literature' 2, 14, 15, 37–9, 41;

landscape writing 5; natural and cultural (Sauer) 16, 69, 144
Lefebvre, Henri 18, 165–6, 168
'literary' and 'actual-world' geographies 115–17, 122–23, combined 31, 73, 94; literal integration of 84, interaction of 10, problematic conflation of 32, 34; and setting 164–5; and the 'spatial hinge' 67
literary cartography, definitions of 20, 70, 86–7, **153–4**; in literary geography 13, 74, 76, Chapter 4 *passim*, 145; in literary studies 7, 153–4
Literary Geographies (bibliography) 11, 64–5, 136, 155
Literary Geographies (journal) 3–4, 11, 19, 53, 64, 79, 135–6
literary geographies 3–4, 11, 13, 22, 59, 71, 143, **154**
literary geography as an academic interdiscipline 1–3, 38–9; as a geographical subfield 2; popular 7, 15–16, 25–6, 33, 101, 143; various definitions of 1–7
literary tourism 73, 116, 135, **155**, and locality 30, 66, 73–4, 115, 155; and popular literary geography 7, 14, 25, 32–3

maps/mapping, Chapter 4 *passim*, **155–6**; literal and metaphorical 7, 20, 70, 76, 86–8; *see also* cartography; literary cartography
Massey, Doreen 42,52, 159, 166; influence on literary geography 42, 58, 60–1, 168; and power-geometry 160–1; and the 'global sense of place' 52, 60, 61, 163–4
metafiction 67, 75, **156**
metageography *see* **imaginative geographies**
metaphor 41, 70, 77, 121, 133, 143, **157**; and cross-disciplinary communication 7, 20, 86–9, 106, 154, 156, 157

modernism 40–1, 67–8, 76, 79, 99, 103, 112
more-than-representational geography *see* **representation**
Moretti, Franco 6, 42

neogeography 104, **158**
new cultural geography *see* **cultural geography**
non-representational theory (NRT) *see* **representation**

online mapping projects 100–103, 129

place 39, 74, 84–5, 102–3, 128–9, **160**; and the event of the text 123; in pre-1990s US literary studies 5, 17; place names 102, 170; **sense of** 45, 52, 60, **163–4**; and spectral geographies 80; writing 'about, for and in place' 51; *see also* **deep mapping**; place writing; Massey, Doreen
place writing 44, 64, 72, 84, 126, 129
Pocock, Douglas C.D. 17, 27, 35, 39–41
poetry 68–70, 95, 124, 125, 129, 134; and American Studies 36; and cartography 98; in ecopoetics **147**; and geographer-poets 68, 69, 72, 125, 142; in the geography classroom 47, 50–1; in geopoetics **151**; and place writing 72; and regional geography 67, 91; as research method 78
positivist geography 36, 40, 90–1, 118, 124, **159–60**; and humanistic geography 151; implicit in GIS 95; post-positivist cultural geography 37, 114
Proust, Marcel 15, 34–5, 116

qualitative methods 45, 78, 91–3, 97–8, 100, 151, 161

region 41, 48–9, 55–6, 66–7, **162**, 111; Canadian 69, 91; and folklore 80; French 31; and regional geography 36, 37, 39, 41, 50, 114–16;

transnational 5–6; UK 32; urban 93; US 31, 91; and the 19th century regional novel 49, 55, 64, 91, 93, 108, 112
relational literary geography 57, 69, 97, 109, 122, 123, **162**
representation Chapter 5 *passim*; cartographic 89–91, 95–6, 99, 101, 155–6; co-productivity of representations and geographies 16, 49, 74, 144, 160; in fan practices 73; and film geography 72; and imaginative geographies 152; of landscapes and the female body 83; literary, of digital technologies 85; and **non-representational theory** / more-than-representational geography 105, 109, 122, **158**; and post-representational cartography 160; of projected landscapes 70; and relational literary geography 162;
Ridanpää, Juha 2, 67, 75, 156, 162
Rossetto, Tania 104–6, 160

Saunders, Angharad 58, 123, 136
scale 42, 67, 84, **164**
science fiction 9, 78–80
setting 30, 35, 72–4, 115–7, 121, **164;** and chronotope 141; Faulkner's 115; generic 81; Hardy's 55–6, 115; Joyce's 121; literary geography 'without settings' 81; Proust's 116; 'reversible' 75–6; *see also* 'literary' and 'actual-world' geographies
Sharp, Joanne 25, 48, 58
Sharp, William 14, 26, 32
short stories 30, 31, 45, 66, 75, 80–82
sky writing 66, 84, **165**
space 165–6, 'container' view of 81, 141, 164, 167; feminist views of 146, 166, 167; *For Space* (Massey) 9, 52, 166; production of 165–6, 168; relational view of 75–6, 97, 99, 109, 122; subjective understandings of 54, *see also* cognitive mapping; spatial metaphors 20, 87, 157
space-time *see* **time-space**
spatial form (Joseph Frank) 15, 33–4, 68, **167**
spatial hinge 67, 123; *see also* 'literary' and 'actual-world' geographies
spatial literary studies 7–9, 18, 21, 131, 143, **169**
spatial turn 10, 17, 35, 53, 90, 149, **168**
spatiality 45, **167;** of literary geography 59–62
spectral geographies 80
story maps 103–4, **168**

Tally Jr., Robert T. 7–9, 131, 147
terminology 20, 70, 86–9, 104–6, 112; importance of clarity in interdisciplinary use of 14, 17, 59, 63; *see also* **cognitive mapping; critical literary geography; literary cartography; maps/mapping**
text as a spatial event 57, 59–62, 78, 80, 97, 123, **168**
Thacker, Andrew 10, 24, 32, 48, 55, 58, 68, 143; and 'the idea of a critical literary geography' 7–8, 10, 18, 24, 101, 126
Thurgill, James 67, 80, 123
time-space 71, 160, 164, **169**
Tuan, Yi-Fu 39, 49–50, 73, 81, 117, 151, 168
Twitter 64, 85

urban 34, 73, 84, 93, 100, 125; and cognitive mapping 88; and cyberfiction 79, and graffiti 84, **literary urban studies 155**; in modernist literature 34, 68; and public transport 51; and Sherlock Holmes 73; Soweto poetry 70–1; and Textopia 100; urban regionalism 66, 93; *see also* city

visual narratives *see* story maps

Watson, J.Wreford (James Watson) 69, 91, 93, 111, 124, 125
Women and Geography Study Group / Gender and Feminist Geographies Research Group 52
Woolf, Virginia 15, 32, 34, 116

Wright, J.K. 27–9, 31, 40, 50, 111; and geosophy 28–9, 117–18, 130, **150**; unsigned essays in the *Geographical Review* 1924–38 15, 30–1, 91, 111; validation of subjective knowledge in geography 28, 37, 114, 117–18

For Product Safety Concerns and Information please contact our EU representative GPSR@taylorandfrancis.com
Taylor & Francis Verlag GmbH, Kaufingerstraße 24, 80331 München, Germany

www.ingramcontent.com/pod-product-compliance
Lightning Source LLC
Chambersburg PA
CBHW071820230426
43670CB00013B/2512